You are all life's meant to be,
a flicker of hope in a desolate sea

For the Love of God

with love & blessings

Jane T.

Jane Thompson (Sri Devi)

 FriesenPress

Suite 300 - 990 Fort St
Victoria, BC, V8V 3K2
Canada

www.friesenpress.com

Copyright © 2016 by Jane Thompson (Sri Devi)
First Edition — 2016

Cover Graphic Designed by Freepik

All rights reserved.

No part of this publication may be reproduced in any form, or by any means, electronic or mechanical, including photocopying, recording, or any information browsing, storage, or retrieval system, without permission in writing from FriesenPress.

ISBN
978-1-5255-0077-0 (Hardcover)
978-1-5255-0078-7 (Paperback)
978-1-5255-0079-4 (eBook)

1. POETRY, SUBJECTS & THEMES, INSPIRATIONAL & RELIGIOUS

Distributed to the trade by The Ingram Book Company

Poems

1	A New Song
3	Angels Galore
5	A Whirlwind Visit
7	A Saint
8	A Time and a Season
10	Acting the Clown
11	Aum
12	Aum Tat Sat
13	Becoming Whole
14	Blessed Master
17	Children of Light
19	Coming Home to You
20	Courage and Faith
21	Glimpses of Life on Psych Ward A2 Lions Gate Hospital, Vancouver, BC
26	Crazy or Not
27	Creatures Divine
29	Deep in Your Heart
30	Endurance and Grace
31	Ever New Bliss
32	Face to Face
34	Farewell My Friends
39	Follow a Master
41	Fools Rush In
43	Salvation
44	Forever Free
45	Fountain of Youth
46	I Had to Find Out
47	Freedom
48	Fruition
49	God's Plan for You

50	Gratitude
51	Greener Pastures
53	Happy Father's Day
54	Harvest Moon
57	He Died for Me
59	He Made it So
60	Heaven
61	Heavenly Light
62	Heaven's Door
64	He's My Brother
65	Holy Spirit
67	Faith in You
68	I Did it for Him
69	It Ain't from the Lord
72	It's All Just a Game
73	It's Up to You
74	Journey's End
75	Joy in Giving
76	Karma's Plight
77	Kriya Yoga
80	Last Night
83	I Wanted Him There
84	Let No Man Get You Down
87	Like a Rock
88	Little Drummer Boy
90	Look for the Good
91	Love Deep as the Pearl
92	Love in His Name
94	Love One Another
97	Lullaby Lane
99	May We be One
100	Meditate on Me
102	Meek as the Lamb
103	Mother Divine

104	My Children's Plight
116	My Companion, My Guide
117	My Faith in the Lord
120	My Guru
122	My Love Affair
127	My Other Sis
130	My Search
133	My Unworthy Gain
134	My Walkabout
138	Never Look Back
140	New Year Dawning
142	One Who Knows Me
144	Only You
147	Onward and Upward
148	Open Our Eyes Lord
149	Our Daily Bread
151	Our Lady of Grace
160	Our Own Demise
162	Peace
163	Pure Through and Through
165	Real Love
167	Road to Glory
169	Satan's Lie
171	Satan's Pleasures
173	Strength and Sight
174	Sweet Mystery
175	Thank You, Dear Master
177	Thank You Sis
180	The Big Chill
182	The Broken Link
184	The Creator
185	The Devil in Disguise
196	The Divine Plan
197	The Dying Game

200	The End of the Line
202	The Forest
204	The Heart is the Knower
205	The Honour of a Father
207	The Lying Game
210	The Master Craftsman
211	The Mountain
212	The Pearl
214	The Poor and the Lonely
215	The Promised Land
217	The Refrain
218	The Seer of All
220	The Spirit Three
221	The Still of the Night
222	The Thrill of it All
223	The White Pearly Gates
225	They're Part of You
227	This Very Hour
229	Those Prison Bars
231	Thou Shalt be Clean
234	Thy Will be Done
235	Together We'll Stand
236	Trust in His Word
240	Trust in You
241	Watching Over Me
242	Way Over His Head
245	When They Reach Heaven
247	You Did it All
249	You Hold Us Dear
250	You'll Never Get Home
251	Your Claim to Fame
252	Your Love
254	Your Smile
255	Your Touch
256	About The Author

A New Song

I wanted a new song
That lights up the hearts
Of my brothers and sisters
Who are lost in the battle
Like wandering cattle
Who are led to the slaughter
And can't even bother
To save their own skin
From the deadlock they're in

They refuse to ask why
All this happens to them
They prefer to do it
Again and again
Never stopping to ponder
What lies over yonder

That bridge to tomorrow
That only brings sorrow
Until we awake
Our will forsake
For a greater plan
One made by the Man

That great being of light
Who'll give us flight
From our own seeming fancy
When we get too antsy

The new song we'll sing
We can't learn it from books
They just dig in the hook
Of pride and intellect
That feed the elect

We can learn it from life
With all of its strife
Then put it to the test
So we can rest
Alone and in silence
Till we hear His guidance
Leading us on
Singing a new song

Angels Galore

You have to fight
For your spirit's redemption
Because God wants
Your abiding attention
To be focused on Him
In order to get in
Let the world pass you by
Spread your wings and fly

He knows all your cares
But He wants you to dare
To leave them behind
He is so kind

He'll soothe your soul
Give you a new role
To play in His drama
Not the one you got
From Mama

Your joy will be full
Your heart content
With everything you need
He'll even pay the rent

With the money you spent
On gifts and toys
They were only Satan's ploys
To keep you bound
On his merry-go-round
Of birth and death
With each new breath

Tarry no more
He stands at the door
Open it up
He'll come in and sup
With His angels galore

Who could ask for more?

A Whirlwind Visit

Now back in Edmonton
Dad once came to visit
With briefcase in hand
You couldn't even zip it.
It was full of hard cash
In case he had to dash.

He took us to supper.
It made quite a flutter.
The waiter came running
Out of the lounge with a sputter:

"Sir, your bill was one hundred,
So why all the clout?
You must have been mistaken,
When you ran out.

"One hundred in a tip?
Surely you've taken a nip!"

"Why, take and enjoy!"
He replied with a cry.
"It's a toss in the bucket;
I tell you no lie.

"Good man, you'll soon find
I'm just a little
Out of my mind."

Then off to the mall.
He hired a cab
To take the kids shopping,
To show he's their dad.

"A watch for my son!
Perfume for my daughter!
What else can I give them
As an absentee father?

"A new coat for winter,
Some boots for their feet,
That certainly would be
A welcome treat."

Then he hightailed it
Out of town with great speed,
Having completed his
Dutiful deed.

A Saint

A saint is a sinner
Who never gave up
Who sits with the Lord
In His kingdom to sup

It's not hard to believe
In a saint you must conceive
If you want to be free
Live eternally

A Time and a Season

Lord, let me not
Get caught in the net
I know it is Satan
On this you can bet

When I feel the pain
Suffer the drain
On my spirit and life
When it is filled
With much strife

Please remind me to pray
To keep the blues away
So I may not stray
From Your harbour of peace
Lord, may I decrease as
You increase

So You will come first
Then my heart will burst
Open with song
I cannot go wrong

In trials we grow
As Your word, You doth sow
In our hearts and our minds
In our praises we'll find
Your promises true
You'll see us through

Give thanks to the Lord
For the plan that He bore
For the good and the bad
Don't look at the sad

Take them as lessons
You needed to learn
Perhaps His refining
You shouldn't spurn

Be glad for the trials
They're meant for a reason
They'll only be with you
For a time and a season

Acting the Clown

God is no weakling
He invented it all
From the grandest to lowest
Scheme of the fall

From grace to perdition
It's a long way down
But you'll only be left
With tears and a frown
For acting the clown

Aum

There is a place
Beyond time and space
A heavenly abode
Where wonders unfold

Where rivers abound
With the roaring sound
Of cosmic Aum
That fills us to the bone

With happiness replete
We feel complete
Aum fills that great hole
Deep in our soul

Aum Tat Sat

When the soul is set free
With the spirit three
Aum Tat Sat
It is that
Which fuels the fire
Of our desire
To find peace and joy
Not be a toy
To our senses and lusts
It is a must
If you want to be free
It takes all three

Becoming Whole

We must become whole
Our eternal goal
One with the Creator
The Lord God above
Who is filled with compassion
And illimitable love

I know I have learned
Your love
Is not to be spurned
We must die to the self
Forsake great wealth
Put them on the shelf
Be born again free
Live life for Thee

Blessed Master

Whenever I see your face
All my fears subside
Whenever I hear your voice
My love I cannot hide

When I look into your eyes
I see the depths of oceans apart
Your piercing gaze goes
Straight through to my heart

Casting all falsehood
Out into the dark
Leading me onwards
To make a new start

Wherever thou wishest
I should go
To learn and be helpful
As I grow

In stature and stamina
So I may endure
Whatever you choose for me
I am sure

That it is the best
For a time and a season
I know that you have
Every good reason

In trusting you
I have been out on a limb
Then you beckon me
"Come back in."

I have to say
Despite the times
That were so tough
You saw me as a diamond
In the rough

I never feel lonely
With you by my side
My joys and my sorrows
I need not hide

You are all
Life's meant to be
A flicker of hope
In a desolate sea

Of shattered dreams
Worn-out crosses
From loved ones and friends
Even our bosses

But you, my guru
Have been faithful and true
Guiding and leading me
All the way through

What more could I ask
Than a master and friend
To see me home safely
Till I reach the end

Children of Light

Lord, teach us to fight
To be children of light
Lord, take hold of us now
Come show us how

Then we'll know what to do
Come what may
With each passing day
The price we must pay

To join in Your army
With sword in hand
Together we'll stand
United in love
Faith, hope, and charity
Where there is no disparity

Where there is no
Richer or poorer
Or greedy old man
Only love and hope
The strength to cope
With all of the trials
That beset us still
Till Your purpose
We fulfill

―――――――――

Let us fight
As children of light
Let them see Your great power
That guides us each hour
Your strength and might
Your wisdom and sight

Coming Home to You

I've learned to take
My stance at last
I know my troubles
They shall pass

In prayer and quiet
In song and worship
I will seek Thee
As my bishop

The one who sits upon my throne
The one who calls me
"Jane, come home."

It's getting easier by the day
Though I may wander
Go astray

With faith to guide me
Love to see me through
I will not tarry, Lord
I'm coming home to You

Courage and Faith

It takes great courage
Willpower and faith
If you want to keep pace
With His laws and His virtues
Respecting His curfews
Of when to act
When to stand still
With none of the frills
That adorned you before
If you want to open
Heaven's door

His kingdom of love
Shines from above
It fits like a glove
That can only be worn
Once we've been torn
From our own selfish ways
Get down and pray
That love may abide
Deep in our hide
Clearing the way
For a brand new day
Filled with laughter
Forever after

Glimpses of Life on Psych Ward A2
Lions Gate Hospital, Vancouver, BC

On Psyche Ward A2
We just sleep and eat
Though some will venture
Out in the street
Others take their coffee breaks
Then there's some
Who find a good mate!

The pj's got
No ribbon and lace
They're all the same
So you're not out of place
When you go outdoors
To see the big dipper
In your pillow-paw socks
Or your blue paper slippers.

The meals are filling
But not too tasty
The cooks don't spice it
For us here crazies.

They don't use salt
But the pepper's free
Sugar's a no-no
While some eat for three.

―――――――

The heat it makes me
Bake in bed
It turns my cheeks
From pink to red
It makes my mouth
And skin so dry
My tongue so rough
That I could cry.

Some folks bum smokes
All day and night
They have no money
So they gotta fight
To get out in the yard
When the shakes set in
They'll take a good Players
Over a bottle of gin.

To see 'em puffin'
Under the wooden gazebo
You know it's for certain
It ain't no placebo.

Then there's the butts
That lots of them smoke
It's a shame; it's a pity,
God knows they are broke.

When pill time comes 'round
The nurses run ragged

After patients who are dozin'
Roamin' or haggard.

The rest all turn
Flee the med scene
Yell and gripe that
They're feeling quite green
From all of the meds
They hate to take
That make them dizzy
Start to shake.

Fat chance they're fake
You can tell by their faces
By the way they act out
By the clues and the traces
That are etched on the door-sills,
The lintels and posts
That are filled with sad memories
Some of the ghosts.

From their broken-down dreams
Their unhealed traumas
Most likely they come from
An absentee Mama.

You pray you won't sleep
In that cell on the floor
With a bottle to pee in
A guard at the door.

You're lucky if you even
Get out for a smoke
It's cold, dark, and lonely
It's no friggin' joke.

The building is old
The pipes they sure show it
They hiss and they sing
Till you think they might blow it.

You gotta' rise early
To get a hot shower
Or you'll come out shivering
Like a frozen, wet flower.

On a clear, frosty morn
In this mountainous town
If you forget to remember
Hey, they've written it down!

The doctors have worked
With the skills they know best
To the left brain, the right brain
You've had all the tests.

One day they will tell you
You're fit for society
If you keep on your meds
And stick to sobriety!

Go ahead and rest up
While you're hanging around
There's no better Psyche Ward
In Van to be found.

So remember your dreams
They're alive so don't wait
You're here for a reason
It wasn't just fate.

Think of the good times
The friendships you made
The music, the laughter,
The bold renegades.

You're here for a short time
Not here to stay
Let's hope that the blues
And the voices will fade.

The angels stand waiting
At the big pearly gates
Say goodbye and farewell
To the old Lions Gate.

Crazy or Not

Crazy or not
You must be caught
In the battle of life
With all of its strife

Choose freedom
Or remain
In the world in chains
It's not so absurd
To believe in His word

The truth is the reverse
Of what you see now
That's why they'll mock you
Call you a fat cow

A fool is the one
Who understands the game
Views good and bad
As one and the same
He's held fast to the truth
From God's cosmic booth

So crazy or not
You will be caught
In God's net in His time
Then you will know
A life Divine!

Creatures Divine

I've travelled the world
Seen faraway places
Some worth remembering
Some left no traces.

The faces of those
Who are etched in my mind
Are those who were kind;
Those who were cruel;
Each made me bow
At God's footstool.

In humble humility,
Praise and thanksgiving,
I saw all were living
According to His will.
He said, "Jane, be still.

"Look upon
Each creature of mine
As one Divine—
My perfect creation;
They too will have
Their moment of elation.

"When they are ready
For total sublimation,
To My holy will."
He said, "Jane, be still.

"Take no thought
For the things that are bought
With silver and gold;
Lo, behold.

"Give thanks for the spirit
You find within.
Be rid of your pride—
Your deep-seated sin.

"Let go of your plans,
Your worldly knowledge.
I'm sending you to college;
In the school of life,
To battle the strife
That besets each man,
When he bends to My plan.

"Then all will be clear;
All you hold dear
Will surely come about.
You'll dance, sing, and shout.

"You'll learn to live
As a creature Divine—
A life sublime
That is in tune with mine.

"Jane, be still.
Tune in to My will."

Deep in Your Heart

It's through trials
That we grow
Or else sink below
The depths of the deep, dark
Night of the soul

Where temptations abound
You can't hear the sound
Of the small voice within
You only know
What's under your skin

But that itch you can't scratch
You never will patch
With words or with books
You need only take a look

To see what's within
It ain't under your skin
It's deep in your heart
That's where it all starts

Endurance and Grace

Though we put up a fight
Each day and night
To have our own way
In God's cosmic play
One day we'll give up
Thank God for the cup
Of trials and tests
Realize we're blessed
With endurance and grace
To keep on in the race

Ever New Bliss

Onwards
I will walk in joy
Knowing
I am just Your toy
That You have made
To play the part
That You planned
Right from the start

Knowing that
Has made life fun
Now I can
Skip and run
For the prize
Of Your heavenly kiss
That final gift
Of Your ever new bliss

Face to Face

You can do it
Just have faith
Depend on His grace
That He will bestow
As you learn to row
Down the stream of dreams
Where all of life seems
To melt into one
Great harmony with Thee
Father, Son, Holy Spirit
The three

The Holy Spirit was imparted
When Christ departed
But was resurrected again
He could not pretend
To be dead in a tomb
He was conceived in the womb
Of a virgin so pure
Of this I am sure

He was given the task
To release us at last
From sorrow and sin
A new life to begin
When we give up the doubt
Reach out to shout
For His saving grace
We'll see Him face to face

Farewell My Friends

Farewell my friends
My family
I hope you'll be
Happy as can be

I'll miss your smiles
Your sweet embrace
But I won't miss
Much of the disgrace

You heap upon me
When I falter or fall
Or when you make me
Feel so small

That I have to crawl
To get back in your life
When I have finished
With all my strife

It broke my heart
To make a new start
But I know in the end
I'll be stronger to defend

The truths that I see
I will not bend
Or make believe
What I should be
When really I'm looking
To fly free

So for now
I must pass you by
While I reach
For Him on high

No time for games
Or impersonations
That only make
For complications

I want to be true
To my inner-self
That I may have put
Upon the shelf

To save face with you
My family, my friends
I did pretend
To be so happy

In your embrace
When all I saw
Was His face
Looking back at me
Calling me to be free

Free from all
My worldly goods
My attachments, my desires
He set my heart on fire

To rest in His tender, loving care
So I may share
In His love and grace
With ever a smile
Upon my face

With nary a worry
On my mind
For in His care
All my needs
I will find

No more to lament
What goods and folk
I left behind
For I will see
How I was blind
To all the illusions

Surrounding me
Like a deep, dark sea

Of people, places, and things
That only bring
More desires
To fuel the fires
Of discontent
Because we're hell bent
On things of the world
Instead of our goal
Of satisfying our soul
With love and devotion
Like a magic potion

To the Lord God almighty
Who gave us birth
From His lofty perch

Now I am grown
New wings have I sewn
To show me new heights
Of His glory and might

I wish you all well
Only time will tell
How the story unfolds
We must be bold

Take up our cross
Sift out the dross
Then head for the hills
Learn to be still

Till we hear His sweet voice
And we have no choice
But to follow Him home
To sit on His throne

Follow a Master

They condemn those who follow
A different religion than theirs
They think they are the heirs
To the only truth they know
But they haven't looked below
The cover of great works
That offer big perks
By well-known masters
Instead they get plastered
In drink and in drama
And blame it on Mama

But never mind 'cause I know
What I learned long ago
The truth is inside
Mine I won't hide
From their fierce looks and words
That are really absurd

It makes for a story
That is an allegory
That will continue to play
In its own special way
In the pages of history
For that is the mystery
They may finally discover
Under one of those covers

Some words from the wise
Whom they have despised
But who made the journey
Not left on a gurney
But transcended the self
Arrived home with great wealth

Greater than any earthly store
For they have opened
Heaven's door
For others to partake
Their souls to forsake

When you hear of the kingdom
That is found from within
If you follow a master
You'll surely get in

Fools Rush In

Only fools rush in
Partaking of sin
Thinking they can win
All the gold in the earth
It is not worth
The price they must pay
They will have to
Give it away.

When death beckons
At their door
They will wonder
What could I have done more?

God's told me be wary
Walk softly through the storm
Satan's ways aren't the norm
But neither are God's
For He sees it all
He knows why they fall.

They'll have a chance
In their next earthly birth
Hopefully be wiser
Know what they are worth.

Gold cannot buy them
Their doorway to heaven
But fools often take it
For the bread and the leaven.

It's sad. It's a pity
They think they're so witty
The truth they will see
When they're down on their knee
When they are set free.

Salvation

With Your blessings in disguise
A plan of salvation
You will devise
One that is destined
Just for me
One that will make me
Happy as can be
Forever after
With joy and laughter
That fills the rafters.

While I am still human yet
The pain and sorrow
I try to forget
But they will soon
Be gone from me
When You come
To set me free.

So in that faith
I'll strive to live
So to others
I may give
Strength in sorrow
Hope for tomorrow.

I'll live just for Thee
Renewed by Your word
In those sacred texts
I can't wait for what's next!

Forever Free

I know You have told me
In secret communion
About our union
When it will be
Just You and me
Forever free!

Fountain of Youth

High on the mountain
There is a fountain
Of youth to behold
As the story is told

It cannot be found
With your nose to the ground
You need to look high
Way up to the sky

Where eagles fly free
With the birds and the bees
Only to alight
To grab a respite

Then on to new flight
That will take them to heights
Never seen before
They have reached the door

Of sunshine and laughter
That soars to the rafters
Where wisdom sings
With a heavenly ring
Of love and good cheer
For whoever draws near

I Had to Find Out

It's all I can do
To sleep through the night
Satan continues
To put up a fight
To win over my soul
He has made it his goal
To bring me to ruin
His fury is brewin'

Deep in my bones
As I try to disown
All that's behind me
Aim to fly free
Live out the life
God planned for me

So I set out at last
To be free of my past
Begin again anew
It was long overdue

Now I am here
Without any fear
Of what will become
Of the life that I've won

A life of contentment
Free of resentment
Hatred and doubt
I had to find out

Freedom

I like my freedom
Never one for the bore
Of security and labouring
Or wanting more

I never was one
For mediocrity
I prefer to fly free
Live happily with Thee

Fruition

For Your name sake
Those many nights
I lay awake
Lest no man I should
Shun or hate

In the end
We're all the same
Though some seek fortune
Peril and fame
Not knowing their worth
Your loving mirth

The path, it ain't easy
But it is when we pray
Barriers start falling
There dawns a new day

The way opens up
We can sit down and sup
With You as our host
It's then we can boast
When we've paid our tuition
We'll be led to fruition

God's Plan for You

All of the trials
And tests we go through
Are meant in the end
To make us all true

To God's given laws
That are without any flaws
They're meant for redemption
Not ill or exemption

First you need eyes
And ears that recall
That still inner voice
When you were small

For angelic He made us
In His image with joy
But lo, man becomes
One of Satan's little toys

Till we weary of the battle
Give up the fight
Only to find Him
At the end of our plight

He was there all the time
Even leading you through
All the joys and the sorrows
He planned for you

Gratitude

At times I have
No words to express
My undying love
For your tenderness

When I have been
Down and blue
You always managed
To forge a way through

All of my darkness
Sorrow and pain
That I might gain
Your promises true
There is none
Quite like you
My beloved guru

We are so blessed
God sent us to you
To lead us through
Our dark days and nights
Our trials and sorrows
To a better tomorrow

Greener Pastures

If you take it real slow
The pearl you will find
The chains will unwind
In His tender care
I beg you to dare

Your dream you will see
Far beyond the seas
Of worry and doubt
You've got to find out

Dare to believe
Have faith in your heart
Before you depart
That's the key to the story
That leads you to glory

If you knew all the effort
It takes to lay down
All the stakes in the game
You'd probably frown

But I tell you it's worth
All of the mirth
You'll get when you're through
It's all up to you

They may call you crazy
But at least you're not lazy
You'll have asked all the whys
The wherefores of life
Learned the purpose of strife

You'll see that the truth
Is not for the uncouth
It's a blessing and honour
Received from the Father
To lead us to pastures
Much greener in time
To His life Divine

Happy Father's Day

You are a very dear father to me,
And because of you
I can fly free.

Free to be who I am at last,
With happy memories
Of my past.

You're a wonder at age 93.
You've taught me well
To be just me.

You set the rules,
But without the scorn.
Now I can weather any storm.

So thank you from my heart today,
For being my dad,
In your own special way!

Harvest Moon

I watched the full moon
Glowing high in the sky
It lifted my thoughts
To heaven on high

I wondered in awe
How it waxes and wanes
As sure as the sun shines
The clouds bring the rain

Just as the sun
Sets deep in the west
So the moon rises
On this you can bet

It casts its soft glow
O'er earth's wondrous maze
His face lights up
With a jovial gaze

It waxes and wanes
In all of its splendour
It rules all the tides
And life's cycles
So we remember

When to plant
When to grow
When to bow down
To its infinite rhythms
It gives us the signs
It's a fact; it's a given

Surely you've seen
His fat cheeks, his round eyes
His big oval mouth
His look of surprise

When the harvest comes due
He changes his hue
From a soft pale white
You see in the night
To a deep golden yellow
Whose glow is so mellow

You'll see him just o'er
The horizon at dusk
Casting his moonbeams
Over all of the dust
In the fields that lay bare
They've cut all the clover
The harvest is over

The wheat has been threshed
The cows have come home
To the barns to be fed
The babies are sleeping
Tucked in their beds

While Mother stays up
In the kitchen to bake
Some bread for the morning
For her family's sake

She won't need to run
To the corner store
The larder will be full
With riches galore
The freezer laden
With all kinds of treats
With pies and breads
And tender, red meat

The cellar will be stocked
With pickles and jams
We'll celebrate Thanksgiving
With a pork hock or ham

As the pale moon hovers
Way over our heads
We'll be tucked in our beds
With a feeling of content
For our labour well spent

He Died for Me

Though I know not yet
The fullness of His love
He has assured me, "Come in."
I will have peace like a dove

Flying high in the sky
All my tears He will dry
With sweet laughter and joy
His gifts I will employ
To use as He wills
For those who are ill
Needy and alone
There will be no stone
Left unturned by His grace
That I will embrace
As each new day I face
With Him as my guide
All my fears will subside
As I seek to abide
In His presence evermore
When He opens heaven's door

For me to sit down
Wear his bright crown
For a life well lived
Giving all I could give
To those that I met
For whom I have wept
For I knew it was true
He would see me through

I'll always remember
Christ died for me
So I could become whole
And be set free

He Made it So

Try and succeed
In your earthly deeds
Till you feel the thrill
Know it's His will
Then self will subside
He will abide
In your heart and soul
He'll make you whole

He'll make ready your flight
You will not fight
As you did before
When love opens
Heaven's door

But you have to have love
That's way far above
Anything you know
He made it so

Heaven

This life was not meant
To be our contentment
So hold no resentment
Of those who have harmed you
Stood in your way
It was only to make you
Get down and pray

For a better tomorrow
A life filled with glee
A life to be lived
In heaven you see
A life that was meant
For you and for me!

Heavenly Light

The good Lord above
Shelters us like a dove
Flying through
The storms in the night
Putting up a valiant fight

That we may regain
What we have lost
He cleans out the dross
Of our lesser desires
So we may aspire
To realms on high
Reach for the sky

Never look back
To be put in the sack
Of worldly woes
That comes from our foes

Who heed not the call
Are chained to the ball
And shackles that hold them
In the dark of the night
From Your heavenly light

Heaven's Door

Someday you'll arrive
At the white pearly gates
You will not have tarried
Or lain in wait

You'll have passed by the stream
The flowers that grow
You'll have watched the warm sun set
Seen the moon's soft glow

You'll have found that the rainbow
Of peace and contentment
Has been beckoning you on
With no resentment

Only faith in His promise
Of what is in store
When you finally reach
Heaven's door

Your mind will have opened
Your thoughts will be clear
You'll love every being
Hold them all dear

To your heart and your soul
They're part of the whole
Of His creation
In every nation

So tarry no more
To reach heaven's door

He's My Brother

They know not where they're headed
On the long journey home
So back in the world
They do tarry and roam
Not taking the time
To go deep inside
Their pain and their sorrow
They think they can hide

Till the dam bursts open
One dark gloomy day
They haven't a clue
Of the price they will pay
For worshipping self
Not serving others

Little do they know that
In Christ, he's my brother
My neighbour, my friend
A child of God
Till the end

Holy Spirit

I know Satan's tricks by now
For You have taught me
How to bow
In prayer when troubles
Come my way
Now all I have to say
Is that You answer when I call
Even though I feel quite small

I know that You are greater than he
Greater than those in the world, you see
For Christ defeated him
On the cross
Now it's You who are my boss

Satan likes to get a word in
Tempt me with his many sins
Things that are opposite
Of Your righteous ways
So the ticket price I'll pay

I'll stay steadfast in my stance
He won't get a second chance
To sway me with his crooked lies
His plans and schemes I will defy
I'll wait till Satan's fire
Doth retire

I won't budge
You are the judge
You've taught me to fight
Not by power, nor by might

By Your Holy Spirit in me
I will be set free

Faith in You

How do I love Thee
Let me count the ways
In humbleness and humility
I reached out each day
For Your guiding hand
So that I can stand

Thou hast taught me to pray
In joy and in sorrow
When I had to borrow
Your love never lessened
You just kept on blessing

Thou hast filled me with hope
Strength to cope
Through all of my trials
Even when I was in denial

You gave me a reason
With every new season
To have faith in You
To see me through
To a new tomorrow
Free from all sorrow

I Did it for Him

Through all my ventures
'Cross the land
I learned to trust
I learned to stand
I learned to lean
On His guiding hand

Through dark days and nights
I learned to fight
With prayer, dance, and song
I knew I wasn't wrong

God knows my soul
He was making me whole
Following the recipe
He made for me
I was able to stand
Tall as a tree

That bends in the wind
But never does break
I did it for Him
Make no mistake

It Ain't from the Lord

I know he told me
This I am sure
You are my "sunshine"
You are the cure
For all my hatred
Pain and sorrow
Please stay with me
Until the morrow

I stayed, I wept
I crawled, I leapt
I begged him to
Give up the drink
Then drugs came along
And he did sink
Deeper and deeper
In the pit of destruction
With little remorse
He had no compunction

There was naught I could do
But kneel and pray
God might show him
The light of a new day

Show him the harm
That he's doing to others
Who have not the strength
To fight with their druthers

He had a twenty-year sentence
He was half the way through
His heart was so hardened
It made us all blue

How can you tell
A man in the pen
That he can start over
Begin life again
With a brand new story
On the right side of the law
Without a gun that
He always need draw

Our troubles we've made
Of our own accord
Don't blame them on Him
They ain't from the Lord

It's a choice that we made
Sometime in the past
Maybe hoping
It wouldn't last

As each groove grows deeper
The well of ill fortune
Becomes our keeper
It gets harder to escape
But it isn't our fate

God made us for righteousness
His purpose and plan
So stand up, straighten up
Like a good, honest man

It's All Just a Game

God created us all
With His plans great and small
We need only look inside
Behind the fears that we hide
They'll always remain
As long as we play in His game

We can never stand still
As He beckons us ever
To new heights and vistas
He is so clever

To tailor our journey
To our own special needs
It is God who is constantly
Planting the seeds

Our successes and failures
They're all just a game
In His remarkable movie house
It's His claim to fame

It's Up to You

We are all used to
Working it through
When really it is
Up to You

To help us, dear Lord
Make us understand
Let us take Your guiding hand

Put away our false pride
Become meek as the lamb
Let us do more for others
Let us do all we can

Let's show others Your love
Your forgiveness and compassion
Even though it seems
Not in fashion

To return good for bad
It is really so sad
To see all the hatred
Jealousy and strife
That have become
A big part of this life

Without You in our hearts
From Your laws we depart
So You must enter in
That's where it begins

Journey's End

You often leave me
In the lurch
Sitting in doubt
Upon my perch

Wondering how
I'll ever get through
Then You touch me
And renew
My faith, my hope
My goal anew

I need not worry
'Bout trials You send
I know You'll be there
At my journey's end

Joy in Giving

In giving we find joy
We're no longer a decoy
One of Satan's toys
Who puts his wealth on the shelf
For a better tomorrow
That may never come
Till our good deed is done

Karma's Plight

When I look up in the sky
So blue, so vast
I see my past
Before my blinded eyes
In the morning sunrise

The evening tide breeze
Oft makes me wheeze
From the trials I bore
As I evened the score
Of my karma's plight
I had to fight
To be free of sin
So You could enter in

Kriya Yoga

Puffed up with pride
They could not hide
The wrongs they've done
All the songs they've sung
'Bout love and affection
Eternal protection
While they turned on their heels
Screeched their wheels
Sped down the road
Leaving you
Carrying your load

On your own once again
To lie and pretend
That their love was for real
It was just their spiel
To serve their own ends
They couldn't make amends

Their hearts were still hard
Like a big lump of lard
That will only melt
When the fire is felt

The fire of affliction
From so much addiction
To this or to that
Or maybe they're just fat
From all of their gluttony
Lust and temptation
Not enough lamentation

For the thoughts and the ways
Of our good Lord above
Who is willing and able
To fill them with love

Which they know not about
Because they haven't stepped out
Of their small minds and ideas
To do their Kriyas

Which would change their ill fate
Take away all their hate
Turn it to gold
So they would behold
His kingdom inside
And there abide

In joy, not in sorrow
They would see that tomorrow
Brings a new dawn and chance
To do a new dance
That lights up their hearts
From His heavenly cart
That is filled to the brim
With great wonders, not sin

Last Night

I talked with You
Again last night;
You never let me
Out of sight.
No matter if
I'm near or far,
You keep me shooting
For the star

Of grace eternal and
Lasting joy;
You can use
Any ploy
To set me right,
When I should stray.
Dear Lord, I thank thee.
This I pray:

"Should I slip
And fall back down,
You'll set my feet
Upon the ground
Of truth and life
And liberty,
Right into the realm
Of eternity."

No friend or foe
Is there around,
When I am soaring
Homeward bound.

For all has melted
In the pot,
Of dreams and hopes
That I have sought;
No longer needed
In the end,
The goal is near,
Right 'round the bend.

A few more steps
Some trials to bear,
Then in Your arms
I will declare:

"'Tis I, dear Lord,
I've reached the end."
You will greet me
As Your friend.

What joy, what peace,
My soul's on fire;
I will have attained
My heart's desire.

Then I'll know
How the story goes,
When all is done,
The battle won.

Until that day
I'll kneel and pray,
With You by my side,
My friend, my guide.

I Wanted Him There

I wanted him there
I could not bear
To see him so lost
At his own cost

His soul was on trial
For his selfish denial
How could I be happy
Knowing he felt crappy
About winning the plot
For my goods that he sought

I stood by and waited
Till the storms abated
In hopes that his soul
Would remake his goal
Of what he was after
The joy and the laughter
That only come in
When we're free of our sin

There was naught I could do
To make him see through
His own selfish ways
The price he must pay
In order to recapture
Life ever after

Let No Man Get You Down

It doesn't matter
What we do,
If we're prepared
To wear the shoe
That fits our soul,
Not make a hole
In our heart and mind;
Always be kind
To those who oppose us,
Not make a fuss
Over trivial matters.
It is a must.

On the long road to heaven,
Just count to seven;
Breathe in life,
Forget the strife.
Let go and ignore
Those terrible bores.

Mankind in a rut,
Living in his hut
Of self-created Hades,
Wondering, "What gave?"

Why do the walls all fall,
When he gets in a brawl?
Only to wake and forsake
His God-given right,
To stand up and fight
For justice and mercy,
For his forsaken soul
That has lapsed in a hole.

A pit of despair
He cannot repair,
Till he forsakes self
And shares his wealth,
Thinks of the other,
Gives thanks and praise
For his Divine Mother,
His Father on high,
With one great big sigh.

Lest he has forgotten
How he was begotten,
God's mighty son
Made in His image
Fit for any scrimmage.

Be it friend or foe,
He has given us a bow
To shoot for the stars;
Never look back
Till we take from our sack
All of the arrows
Of self-abnegation
And that loathsome resignation.

That we are not fit
To wear the crown,
Of wit and wonder,
Let no man put you asunder.

Worthy, He made us
To wear a smile not a frown;
Let no man ever
Get you down.

Like a Rock

Through scenes of darkness
Wide and deep
At home alone at night I weep
For my weary friends
And foes
That I may take
Some of their blows

You have built me
Like a rock
Upon which I stand
Some people mock

In bewilderment they wonder,
"What, has she gone asunder?"
But lo, You pulled me through
That they may have life
Live it for You

Little Drummer Boy

Lord, how my heart aches
For those lost, lonely souls
Who blaspheme Your name
While they play in Your game

They think they know all
But they're really quite small
Those know-it-all kings
With the bad tidings they bring
Of doom and destruction
Wars and strife
They think that's life

Blaming it on You
They haven't a clue
Of the world You created
They are so sated
With all their self-knowledge
They haven't been to college
To learn justice or truth
From Your cosmic booth

They don't know of Your plan
For each and every man
They just take what comes
Act real dumb
Forgetting to pray
For Your wisdom and truth
They speak so uncouth

They will not refrain
From mocking Your name
Your ethics and morals
They keep up the quarrels

They know not the rules
They are just fools
Who think they are kings
A different song they all sing

Than Your little drummer boy
Who had no decoy
Other than faith in You
To see him through

Look for the Good

Look for the good
Instead of the bad
It's only your attitude
That's driving you mad

When you really look under
You will discover
That all the illusions
Have been torn asunder

You needn't make faces
For the wrongs
Or the places
That you've been
In your life
That are causing you strife

You need only look deeper
To see who's the keeper
Of your bad thoughts
And temptations
All the sensations
That come passing through
It ain't God, this is true
It's none other than you!

Love Deep as the Pearl

Through thick and thin
I walked around
On rocky ground
With not a sound
But Your sweet voice
Leading me on
Homeward bound

At times I was
In such a swirl
Whirling with love
Deep as the pearl
That can only be found
In communion with You
My Lord,
You always pulled me through

Wishing and hoping
I could pass it on
That love so deep
For those to keep
Inside their hearts
And minds forever
Remembering You
In their endeavour

Love in His Name

Nothing can hurt you
Though others desert you
With God on your side
In his presence abide
By day and by night
Keep Him in sight

Let no sorrow affect you
No words cut through
Just carry on serving
Loving Him too

He knows what's best
He'll never stop putting
Your soul to the test
Till you learn to be still
Give up your will
Know He is God
To whom you should nod
And worship instead
Of what's in your head

For the mind is a tool
We used in school
But His lessons learned
Can only be earned
By opening your heart
On that great journey depart

For pastures unknown
Once the seed is sown
Never looking for results
Or at all the insults
You'll get on the way
That's the price you must pay
For doing His will
While time there is still

The road, it is long
The mountain's high
If you want to draw nigh
To His loving presence
It is the essence
Of all of our striving
Our hopes at arriving
At that eternal goal
That will make us whole

God's not looking for gain
Just your love in His name

Love One Another

How can you take Jesus
As your saviour and then
Not help out your neighbour
Your son or your friend?

I've seen them do it
Time and again
Just love you and leave you
To sort out and fend
For yourself while they sit
On their throne of glory
Thinking they have the only story

I don't think that Jesus
Loves only the Christians
His life was inscribed
With an honourable mission

He cannot be bribed
He will not bend
He came to teach us
To love till the end

To love one another
Till death do us part
It's a love that comes only
From a pure, taintless heart

I'm afraid theirs are punctured
With many a hole
They make citing scriptures
Their highest goal

They say, "Just believe
You'll be saved,
Or you'll go to your grave."
But instead they become
Their very own slave

A slave to such dogma
That starts many a war
They're blind to the truth
Want to settle the score

Between warring factions
By closing the door
Of their minds to the truth
That Jesus did show
Love one another
Even your foe

We all fall short
Of the glory of God
But He has given us
Feet that are shod
With His gospel of love
Deep in our hearts
From His words and His deeds
We must not depart

But over the ages
The truth has been lost
By biblical scholars
The message has been crossed

Mixed with man's
Own personal zeal
Instead of keeping it
Simple and real

The truth of it all
Is really quite small
But man seeks to make it
A complicated game
In His Holy name

All we need know
To keep us in tow
Is to love one another
Even your foe

Lullaby Lane

I'm tired of being treated
Like a nut in shell
When truly I feel
Gloriously well

You've brought me up
Out of the depths
Of torment and pain
It's their loss, my gain

You have written
Your truths in our heart
As it was in the beginning
It was from the start

Most men have taken
Your word with such ease
Then gone and done
Whatever they please

Ignoring their conscience
With a repugnant look
They've even taken
To writing their own books

On man-made laws
Truths and inventions
Then gather together
And call it a convention

My soul is weary
My body scared and bruised
But nary did I linger
Thinking life was a cruise
Down Lullaby Lane
I fought in Your name

I fought long and hard
Through many a plight
Those times I was frightened
I just kept You in sight

I know my trials
Have not been in vain
I hear Your sweet voice
Calling my name

May We be One

As I lay me down to sleep
I pray the Lord
My soul, please keep
Safe in the shelter
Of Your loving embrace
So that I may see You
Face to face

That's all I live for
My dream's dream is done
As I finish my journey
Here on earth
May we be One

Meditate on Me

If you learn to meditate
You can and will
Alter your fate
Because you will find
When you peel back the rind
The pearl within
That will free you from sin

It will erase those old groves
Create pathways that prove
That it works like a charm
Without any harm

Just tenacity and will
To sit very still
Calm the chatter within
As you begin
To listen to Him
Learn of His ways
Then no more will you play
In Satan's game of charades

Of profit and loss
You'll clean out the dross
Sift the dust from the gold
Then lo and behold
You'll enter new life
One with less strife

Sit still awhile
Learn to smile
Go deep within
That's where it begins
Meditate on Me
If you want to be free

Meek as the Lamb

It's called love and truth
From God's cosmic booth
Projected on earth
When He gave us birth

Spiritual freedom
From the bondage of dogma
Custom and race
He gave us His grace
At a time and a place
When we were lost
He didn't count the cost

Christ gave us His love
Took all the shoves
Turned the other cheek
Acted real meek

Meek as a Lamb
Going to the slaughter
He was one with the Father
So didn't bother

He knew His reward
Was one in accord
With God's Divine plan
To save every man

Mother Divine

She'll keep you in tow
In the very first row
Of God's cinema theatre
Where there you can greet Her

Our Mother Divine
Who created the climb
All the beautiful scenes
In your life
While She bore your strife
So you could enjoy
All of Her toys
Until you're fed up
Beg to sup
With our Father, Mother
Friend, beloved God
On whose earth you have trod

We must treat Her with kindness
The earth too feels our pain
She cannot remain
Sunken in wars
For selfish gain

Give thanks for Her blessings
And don't go on messing
With Her beautiful world
Or it will come unfurled

My Children's Plight

He didn't like himself;
A pity!
But boy, oh boy
He sure was pretty.

All the women
Flocked to him.
He didn't mind;
He still was grim!

He felt such a bother
To his loathsome father,
Who never gave him
The time of day,
Though he said,
"I'll pay!"

Instead he buried
Himself in his bed;
He even lost
The hair on his head.

For what's one to do,
When you ain't got a shoe
Without big holes?
So he made no goals

That he could accomplish
In any short time.
His father never had a dime,
To buy him a coffee,
A doughnut or two—
Never mind a shoe!

He rarely ate
His meals at the table;
He always had
An excuse or a fable,
To make us believe
He could not achieve
Those dreams that he had.
He thought he was bad

From the years of berating
From his father's foul mouth,
When he'd yell,
When he'd curse him,
From the north and the south.

I stood by and watched
My son at death's door.
When his battle began
I wondered,
What I could do more.

The drugs, how they held him,
Like a man bound in chains;
I thought he would never
Ever be sane.

His father just laughed
Said he'd teach him 'bout life
In the real world of crime,
If he wanted to know strife.

My daughter hurt too
For what he put her through.
It didn't matter where
He was in the world,
He always had women,
Ignored his little girl.

Who reclined in her bed
Wishing she were dead,
From all his abuse.
She too thought,
"What's the use?

"If only he'd been there,
I wouldn't feel the shame."
Instead her poor daddy
Kept up the lying game.

"I'll be there on Sunday
Or Monday if late."
Instead he bought whisky
To subdue his fate.

The story's the same one
Year after year,
But now it's back
To a bottle of beer.

"Never mind," is the thing
That my children both say.
"Someday he will pay.
He has promised us thus,
So don't make a fuss.

"You can't blame him
For trying."
But in the bottle
He's crying
For those lost years he spent;
On hell he was bent.

"We can only be thankful
For what our mother did earn.
But even at that,
He had the gall to spurn
Her undying efforts,
To put us through school,
And make us believe
In the golden rule:

"'Do unto others,"
We would hear her say,
"Because you never know
When there'll come a day,
When you'll be in need
Or maybe without,
They'll come along,
To help you out.

"Never forsake
Your neighbour or friend;
Be true to them always,
Till the bitter end."

Now that I'm older,
Their burdens I can shoulder
Much better than when I
Was trying to survive
Just to keep alive.

After all of his violence
From all the abuse,
I too used to think,
"What's the use?"

Then again
It's partly my fault.
I needed some Gestalt
Or psychotherapy for the pain;
I could not remain
In this deep, dark sea.
I needed to be set free.

I see them now,
As they hide under their covers.
I know what's inside;
It's the sixth sense of a mother.

To heal them, I've tried;
So many tears I have cried.
I nearly lost hope
When the dam opened and broke,
I couldn't cope.

Then along came a friend
To see to my need,
He believed he could help me,
And he did indeed.
He set me back upon the path,
Of hope and faith,
Of God's good grace.

Still my children,
They did suffer;
I was no more
Than just a buffer.

For the heartache and pain
That still did remain
Deep in their hearts,
I could not impart
The truth of the story.
It was too gory
For their tender ears.
It would only create fears.

It would be too much too handle.
It would snuff out their candle,
Create much despair.
Their father wouldn't be there
By their side anymore,
If God decides
To even the score.

They were too young to know
That in each new life we grow,
In stature and love,
Like the good Lord above.

All that they see
Is what you and me
Do to each other,
When we hide and we cover
Our sins and omissions
Of loving each other,
Just like a dear mother
Does for her child.
So by their side
I'll abide,
Till the Lord moves me on
Singing a new song.

Then again
Dad's back in the pen,
He has all of those folks
With whom he can joke,
'Bout the laws of society.
Mocking sobriety.

They can blaspheme the Lord.
Admit they are bored.
But never confess
They made quite a mess.

Their hearts they may lose
Because they did not choose
Him over money,
Fortune, and gain.
They preferred
The cheating game.

Cheating their family
Out of their good fortune.
Instead they preferred
A new Aston Martin.

"Never mind," I say,
"I will struggle to pay
In my own way
For our food and our shelter
Though it seems helter-skelter.

"I shall recover,
Collect all my druthers
From all the trauma,
The heartache, and pain,
Until at last I can regain

"My strength and my life,
With less trouble and strife.
I'll reclaim my honour;
Look over yonder."

God's seen me through
More times than I can count,
While on his shoulders
I did mount
Up to the peaks
Of mountains so high,
At times I thought
That I could fly.

When the joy did not last,
I had to hold fast
To His promises true:
"I'll see you through!"

It tore a hole in my soul,
And made a great hole
Of worry and doubt,
When I heard my children shout:

"What's the use?
It's no good!
Though you stood
Your ground,
Didn't make a sound
When we quarreled and fought.
Our very lives you bought
With your blood, sweat, and tears,
To ease all our fears
Of what we'd become,
Instead of just bums
Who hang on the street corners,
With all the mockers and scorners,
To fetch a hot meal
Or strike a drug deal."

God has promised,
Come what may,
By their side He will stay;
So I can go on,
Knowing they too are pawns
In His cosmic show.

I need not know
All the whys and the wherefores
Of His great earthly novel;
They won't need to grovel
In the mire and the dust.
It's a given I trust.

His great wisdom and plan
For each beloved man
That He has created
For His own use.
There is no excuse
For us to renege,
Crawl, and beg,
For His loving kindness
Is always behind us.

As we live by His Word,
Don't act like a nerd,
Strive for perfection,
Accept other's rejection;
Have faith in His promise,
His wisdom so true.
He'll see us through.

My Companion, My Guide

Though I should linger in the dark
My faith it doth deepen
Each time I embark
On a new road to freedom
With You at my side
My friend, my lover
My companion, my guide

My Faith in the Lord

My mother, I thought,
Was some kind of a witch,
Who had cast on me a spell
Like a terrible bitch.

Not true I now know
But then it seemed so,
For my childhood was fraught
With much heartache and pain,
And here I was close
To her side once again.

It only brought memories
Of the tears that I shed,
Lying and crying
At home on my bed.

Night after night,
When I was young,
I was glad of the scriptures
To which I clung.

When she called me a tramp,
Then sent me to camp,
"You hate me," I cried;
She was quite the spy.

Watching and checking
My every move;
I became quite a liar,
With a tongue that was smooth.

My days led to weeks
Without any end,
Not even allowed
To go just 'round the bend.

To visit my friends
Or the local drugstore,
Life was a drudgery
And certainly a bore.

For what young girl
Can stay home in her room,
Or spend her time cleaning
With a mop and a broom.
Washing and ironing
While her friends are at play.
That gave me a reason
So I learned how to pray:

"Lord, get me out of here,
Out on my own
So I can live life and
Not feel so alone."

My troublesome teens
Were fraught with much strife,
I wasn't allowed
To have a young adult life.

Then I married a man
Who was intolerant and cruel;
You had to live by his strict rule
Or he was violent and mean.
So I fled the scene.

As I got older,
I couldn't shoulder
The traumas that lay
Deep in my mind
So I had to find
A way to survive
That would keep me alive.

I turned to the Lord;
I believed it was true,
If I kept faith in His promises
He'd see me through.

My Guru

I have a true friend
Whom they didn't acknowledge
He took me to college
I got a degree
In how to be me
Now I'm happy as can be

He taught me great things
From his secret store room
My life and my habits
He did groom
He fashioned me into
A lady of worth
He gave me great mirth

He's bigger than life
But doesn't feel the strife
He's a master of the game
Who didn't seek fortune
Fancy or fame

Just to lend a hand
To his fellow man
Show them the way
That would make each new day
Happy and healthy
Prosperous too
He knows what's good for you

He's one with our Father
In heaven above
Filled with overflowing love
And compassion too
For our worldly plight
He'll teach you to fight

Though it may be through dark
And treacherous nights
He knows your plight
Better than you
He'll see you through

Just surrender your all
Even when you fall
He'll lift you up
Once again in his time
To a life sublime
He is so Divine
My guru, my lover
My friend till the end

My Love Affair

We were living
In a farmhouse
On Rang Thivierge
I was kneeling and crying
Saying my prayers

I know the Lord heard me
He answered my plea
He gave us a home
And a new family

Of wonderful neighbours
And friends who spoiled us
They saw to our needs
And did many fine deeds

Then I met a new man
Who was tall, dark, and handsome
He seemed willing to pay
A very high ransom

To rescue me out of the depths
Of my sorrow
He gave me hope
For a better tomorrow

His hair, it was long
Nearly down to his waist
Not a wrinkle or blemish
Could be seen on his face

That shone like the sun
Shining high in the sky
He whispered sweet love songs
That often made my cry

He held me real close
I felt dearer than dear
He was such an angel
That I had no more fear

He set us up
In a new home
In the valley
Around the hearth
We all did rally

He worked very hard
From morning till night
I never had to
Put up a fight

There was food on the table
A car at the door
I didn't have to walk
To go to the store

I'm sure it was lust
That kept him in sight
But one day I gave him
A terrible fright

When I told him
He'd be sleeping
In the room 'cross the hall
He got down on his knees
And started to bawl

"I love you my darling,
Just one last time in bed
It's not such a sin."
He was out of his head

"I'll marry you anyway,
Take you to the altar.
Then surely you'll welcome me
And I won't falter."

"Yes," I said firmly,
"When the ring's on my finger.
Until then I shall not
Dally or linger."

He wasn't too happy
Sleeping alone
One morning I saw him
He looked like a clone

Like some "dead man"
I saw walking
Straight down the hall
No longer was he
Handsome and tall

The ghost I saw hidden
Inside of his heart
Had hightailed it out of there
With one great start

I think he praised beauty
But the beast he did fall
Just like Humpty Dumpty
Right over the wall

The guilt was too much
For he had a wife
Back home in New York
Who gave him great strife

Our stories were similar
So much the same
Except that his wife
Came running again

Right into our house
Right up to our door
It was early one morning
I nearly fell on the floor

For a while it was just
The two of us
Making a fuss
About who'd be mistress
To satisfy his lust

One day I came home
From my job in town
And he was wearing
A great big frown

"I'm leaving," he said.
"I've stripped off my bed.
My boxes are packed.
There's no clothes
On the rack."

I couldn't believe
What he had up his sleeve
One day he was professing
His undying love
The next day he was gone
Flying free as a dove

My Other Sis

My other sis
I sure do miss
For we were always
Close as friends
She vowed she'd be there
Till the end.

Till Satan came along that day
Put a knife between the rays
Of sunshine and laughter
That we shared
Our lives, our journey
We always compared.

As we travelled the road
Each one in her city
Now it's such a gall-darn pity
Because she thinks
I'm going to hell for my treason
I'm not sure I can fathom
Her rhyme or her reason
I've got the wrong Jesus?

She curses and gripes
About hatred and strife
That everyone's evil
That she has no life.

Most of her friends
Have deserted her path
Because of her hatred
And deep-seated wrath
Her spiritual pride
That won't let you in
She thinks you are rotten
Stinking with sin.

I've taken her in
To my home in the past
And try as I did
To make it last
She always found fault
With all whom she met
That weary was I
No rest could I get
From all her complaining
About people and things
That at times
I wished I had wings
To fly to some corner
Where she could not reach
Where she could not preach
About Jesus, her saviour
While she did screech
Or hide in her room
In all of her gloom.

She's daring enough
To write me her stuff
Telling me well
I am going to hell
Because I do Yoga
And meditate
She says that's my fate
She can't wait.

I no longer believe her
That I'll die in my sin
Because Jesus still loves me
And beckons, "Come in."

I have faith in His wisdom
I don't lean on my own
I know He has promised
To carry me home.

My Search

I was searching and searching
For that peace that surpasses
All the mad crowds and masses
Who create the brawls
Make you crawl
To get their attention
A helping hand
Instead they drive you
Out of the land.

With their pride and fear
You dare not come near
Or you will be taken
Into their net and forsaken
For some crazy lady
Who's gone 'round the bend
With her tests and her trials
They'll say you're in denial.

The facts are all there
Though they cannot bear
To look truth in the face
You just become a disgrace.

They put you asunder
So they can rob, pillage, plunder
What they value most
And it ain't the Holy Ghost!

But never mind it all
I've had many a fall
But got back up
With the Lord to sup
Drink from His cup
Of love and mercy
His tender care
So that I can bear
Whatever He sends
I need not pretend
To be glad when I'm sad
Or safe when in trouble
But they want to
Burst my bubble.

Drag me down
To look like a clown
When all that I need
Was a friend in good stead.

Who would help me instead
Of making a bed
Of thorns and rose bushes
With their shoves and their pushes
That only broke me some more
While I lay on the floor
With such heartache and pain
I vowed, never again.

―――――――――――

But still I don't hate them
Just pity their stance
I prefer to laugh, sing, and dance
I've been given the chance
To start out anew
Make my dream come true.

But they knew it not
Because they never sought
To ask it of me
I wanted to be free
I wanted to be me.

My Unworthy Gain

For love
I will gladly suffer
If it means
I can be a buffer
For those who know not
They are caught
In the web of delusion
Of life's profusion

Of the myriad games
Self plays for its gains
And not for the other
Not even his mother
Who bore him in body
Soul and sound mind
Hoping he'd be kind
To his neighbour and friend
His sister, his brother
His many others

I've been there myself
Put the other on the shelf
So I could win out
Dance, sing, and shout
But all the while
I could not smile
Because I was in pain
From my unworthy gain

My Walkabout

One day I set out for "Fresno Bay"
For three day and nights
I wandered like a stray
I didn't sleep. I didn't eat.
Till I couldn't stand upon my feet.

My ankles swelled up,
Like balloons filled with water;
I became so confused
That I teetered and tottered.

It was a weird, mystical spin
Of wandering days,
Long, lonely nights;
Most of the time
I was out of sight.

Wandering the streets
For hours and hours,
With tears and fears
And muddle galore;
I'd never been
Like this before.

I wound up at the airport,
Tried to get a flight,
But security found me
And gave me a fright.

They hauled me off
To the psyche ward in town;
With straps and with force,
They couldn't keep me down.

My voices were saying
That I'd be resurrected,
If I just got run over,
I'd surely be ejected

Into the heavens above
So great was my love
For the Lord at that time,
It didn't seem like a crime

To stand in the car park
With cars passing by.
"Just hit me!" I cried.
Then I would fly
Back to the earth,
In a puff of great smoke.
That's what I was thinking;
It was no joke.

Up on the psyche ward,
The days were a frenzy,
With all of us shouting,
Laughing, and pretending.

―――――――

I flushed my pills
Down the toilet each day,
Praying, "Lord get me out of here;
Show me the way."

They treated me nice,
But it didn't suffice
To make me feel better,
Though I obeyed to the letter.

So in flew my father;
I'm sure it was a bother
To miss his golf game,
Or cadets, or another
Lady he was courting,
Because he was snorting:

"Jane, what in heavens
Happened to you?
You're not the same girl
That I once knew."

I, too, knew him not,
Because I was so fraught
With pills and anxiety.
My vision was blurred.
My speech was all mumbled;
I couldn't say a word.

He flew me home
Back to Edmonton town,
Shaking his head
With a great big frown.

The doctor's report
Said it was all in my brain.
"Schizo" they called it;
Some say "insane."

Try as they might,
They couldn't discover
The right pill for me;
So they kept trying others.

Till one day I found
One I could stand
Or take the reprimand
From my mother, who said:

"Dear, what's a pill
For the rest of your life,
Compared to you living
With all of this strife?"

But I didn't believe them;
I was fine in my head.
It was just the old memories
Of the bad times instead.

Never Look Back

Never look back
Put your hand on the plough
The time to seek God
It is nigh; it is now!

Cry no more tears
Let go of your fears
It was all for a reason
Just for a season.

Soon you'll be resting
In God's sweet abode
Of love and of joy
Of blessings untold.

God is the treasure
You surely will find
When you look straight ahead
Instead of behind.

There are no mistakes
That He cannot pardon
He invented them all
In His playhouse and garden.

Weep not for family
Friend or foe
For goods and possessions
That just come and go.

Just thank Him
As you go to sleep
Pray the Lord
Your soul to keep.

For the prize of His
Eternal bliss
Is something you won't
Want to miss.

New Year Dawning

A new year is dawning
But everyone's yawning,
Feeling tired and bored,
Because they haven't scored
In the game of life;
They see only toil and strife.

They haven't the tools
That'll give them the jewels
Of a new life Divine,
A new ladder they must climb.

The stairway to heaven
Is fraught with great danger.
It's a life that was lived
By a babe in a manger.

Still they look yonder
To paths near and far,
Instead of following
That great, bright star

That can be seen in the darkness
Inside the forehead,
That star that will lead them
To heaven instead.

They rely on conditions
That lay 'round about them
Instead of asking,
"Where, why, and when?"

If only they'd pray
For His will to be done,
Instead of wandering
Like a long, lost son.

The answer may come
Like a burst of sunlight,
Illumining the mind
With a terrible fright.

If they will follow,
Obey His Divine Will
Instead of sitting still,
The treasure they will find
Is a life lived sublime.

One Who Knows Me

I know there are those
Who are content with their lot
They know not the plot
That's been designed just for them
They prefer the playpen.

Four walls and a door
With their meal on the floor
Sitting and begging
For each little crumb
Pretending they are dumb
Unable to stand
With His sword in their hand.

They labour and strive
Just to stay alive
When He stands at the door
Beckoning, "Come in.
Sit down at my table;
I'll free you from sin.

"Sin for forgetting
I am here by your side.
You cannot hide
From your small, narrow view;
I've given you life,
Made you brand new.

"So why be content
With the crumbs on the floor?
I came to offer you
So much more.

"Get up, take your cane,
Open your eyes and refrain
From licking the dust.
Be free, you must!

"The beggars, the lame,
The rich, and the poor,
They're all just the same,
But one who knows Me,
Is bound to be free."

Only You

*(In memory of my lifelong friend, Marilyn,
with deepest love and gratitude. I will miss you)*
August 23, 2014

Only you
Could have known my heart
You sensed its calling
Right from the start
That day I walked you
Home from school
That "new girl" in town
Who was so cool

You must have known
What lay ahead
Because through the years
You were my head,
My hands, my heart
To lead me through
A shoulder to cry on
When I was blue

Joy and laughter
We often shared
We danced and cheered
We were quite a pair

Can hardly remember
A day we were apart
Laughing or crying
Baring our hearts

Oh, how I've thanked God
That He did send
A companion, a confidant
Such a good friend

Who stood beside me
Throughout the years
You soothed all of my sorrows
Took away my fears

With compassion and grace
Such wisdom so true
I dare not think
Where I'd be without you

I owe my good fortune
To you, my dear friend
For having stood by me
From beginning to end

I'm sure that you sensed
I was well on my way
After painstaking years
There dawned a new day

A life of good fortune
Love and good cheer
Please know it's because
You loved me so dear

I send you great thanks
For your love so tender
I hope the good Lord
Will always remember
The good you have done
For your family and friends
Only you could have done
What you did till the end

Onward and Upward

He's fashioned each day
With sunshine and rain
To soothe all our pain
Wash away troubles
Make life a dream
Like a swift flowing stream

Stay rooted and steadfast
Like the soft moonbeam
That appears in the night sky
As you look up high

Then sure as the daylight
Of each dawning day
Comes our way
"Press onwards and upwards"
I heard Him say

Open Our Eyes Lord

Open our eyes and ears to see
That life was meant
To be lived for Thee

Let us see all the beauty
We have inside
So we don't have to hide
Behind praise and demands
And others commands

That's what we were taught
When we were in school
But we must live
By the golden rule

There is a way
That You have laid out
All we need do is
Sing praises and shout

Praise God for his goodness
He's within and without
He knows what life
Is all about

Our Daily Bread

God gives me what I need each day
He has taught me how to pray
First I tell Him of my love
Because He watches
From above
He has saved me
From great sin
I cannot help
But let Him in

The sin that begets most men today
Is that they forget to pray
For guidance and His loving grace
For each new day that
We must face
Not knowing where
It leads us to
But when we pray
He leads us through

How else can we
Expect to stand
Journey to
The Promised Land

At home alone
We must kneel and pray
For Him to guide us
On our way

For on our knees
The world gets bigger
Than just this little lump of sugar
That we drop into our cup
Each time we wake
And when we sup

As each new day
Draws to an end
By my bedside
I like to bend
To thank Him for
His care so tender
There's nary a day
Or night I remember
Not talking to Him
From the depths of my heart
That I should not stray
Nor ever depart
From His strong hand that guides me
To my journey's end
He's my Lord, my companion
My lover, my friend

Our Lady of Grace

*(Inspired personal message received from my beloved
Guru, Paramahansa Yogananda)*

Son, let me tell you
'Bout our lady of grace
You're sitting and staring her
Right in the face.

She's so kind; she's not cruel.
She lives by the golden rule.
"Do unto others,
As you'd have them
Do unto you."
She's been to life's greatest school.

One of hard knocks, hardship, and pain,
But the lessons she's learned
Have not been in vain.

She triumphed in each
Seeming impossible feat
She smiled all the while
At each person she'd meet.

Never showing the fear,
The tears that she cried;
In order to do so,
She sometimes had to lie.

You see,
There's a difference

'Tween a truth and a lie
You'll learn son, to know it
When you reach up on high.

Laws were not written
For us to disgrace;
Honor and justice
Are written on our face.

I've seen her walk into
A crowd like no other;
She held her head high
Just like her mother.

She wore that bright gown
Of great honour and grace,
With a twinkle in her eye
And a smile on her face.

Wouldn't you too,
If you knew what to do
On your journey through life,
With all of its strife.

Even though you were shaking,
Had to pretend you were faking,
From everyone's making
Of such hatred and lies.

She's become like a goddess,
One of God's spies,

Who routes them all out
When they scream and shout,
"She's gone mad!
She's gone crazy!"
When all the while
They were just lazy.

Too lazy to ask
All the questions in life.
She asked them all
And was given much strife.

But all of her searching
For answers you see
Has made her steadfast,
Tall as a tree,

That bends in the wind
But never does break.
She's made of God's love,
Her life would forsake

For some lonely straggler
She's met on the way;
She'd take him and care for him,
Give him a bed.
Soon he'd be new again,
Restored and fed.

But that's not all
When she answered the call
To take up her cross,
Follow Him alone,
She gave up her home
To strangers from near
And faraway lands,
Who buried their heads
Deep in the sand
Of ignorance and bliss,
For only a kiss,
While she hid her sorrow
For a better tomorrow,

Which she knew had been promised
In those great scriptures she read.
She memorized verses
She practiced instead
Of giving into trials
Or lying on her bed.

She carried the burdens
Of others less fortunate;
She walked in their shoes.
She paid their dues.
So they never knew
Of the burden she bore,
Of wrongs and of rights,
She never kept score.

Only gave them her love,
In return for a slap
She held them so tightly
On her big, soft lap.

Even though her journey
Is drawing to an end
I know she won't tell you
Of the help she would lend.

Nobody knows
Of the kingdom she'll inherit.
He has a mansion for her,
One of great merit.
One she deserves
For the lives she's preserved.
But they knew it not,
Because they were so fraught
With anger and guile
When she'd only smile.

Tell them she loved them,
Show no ill will
Even when they made her
Swallow a pill.

To still all those voices
She heard from above,
She was doing it for me, dear ones
Out of sheer, utter love.

And not without trembling,
Trouble and pain.
She knew her reward
Would not be in vain.

Once ego's gone,
We become just a pawn,
In God's play on this stage
Who is to gauge?

What's right and what's wrong?
They know not His wishes.
They all swim like tadpoles,
Instead of like fishes.

Many an underground
River she swam.
She walked like a lady,
Fought like a man.

She sometimes slid,
When the pills she hid,
To hear like before
His knock on the door.

For when He comes calling,
We all should be crawling
On bended knee,
To see under the tree
Of life with its riches,
Its hidden treasures
That no one can learn,
No one can measure,
By any of the books
They have on the shelf,
The knowledge is hidden
Deep in the self.

It illumines our minds
Like a thief in the night,
Sometimes it can give us
Quite a fright.

She stood out in the cold
Hard light of the day,
Was prepared to pay all
Give all away.

For we came here with nothing,
With nothing we leave,
Except for the truths
We wear up our sleeves.

The road ain't for sissies
The proud and the old;
It's meant only for those
To whom truth's been told.

Then there are those
Whose eyes have been blinded,
By self-righteous pride;
They keep might on their side.

Their ears have gone deaf
From the din and the noise
Of listening to gossip,
Rumours, not poise.

There's nothing more sacred
Than a mind that can reason
That we don't learn
In one short season.

Trudge on my dear brothers,
My sisters, my friends,
Maybe you'll catch up to her
Before her journey ends.

As for Me,
I have taken
Her words and her deeds,
Placed her here safely
In my home with her needs,
All taken care of
Along the way,
Because she knows how to
Get down and pray.

To the one who has given her
Joy and great sorrow,
It's all in the book, you'll read
Some tomorrow.

Until then, my dear son
Your journey's just begun.
Tarry no more;
He stands at the door,
Knocking and praying
You'll sit down and sup,
Receive His great love,
Never give up
Till you find Him too,
And He makes you brand new.

Our Own Demise

We're our own demise
The devil in disguise
But when we're ready
For the rap
We'll get out of the trap
And do unto others
Without our own druthers

When we open our hearts
There begins a new start
Down the long road to freedom
From profit and gain
We'll see each other
As one and the same

We'll give thanks instead
To the one who is head
Of our earthly sojourn
Then He will adjourn
Our journey for us
Without too much fuss
Just a simple goodbye
From His throne in the sky

He'll carry us yonder
To new heights to ponder
The next stage of life
That is freer from strife

As each step we take
Our journey He'll make
Much sweeter to climb
To His life Divine

Peace

Peace is the treasure
You surely will find
When you are living
Marching in time
With His footsteps that run
Like a faithful son
Up the road in time
With His will, not thine

It's not just a notion
It's a magical potion
Peace can be achieved
If you really believe

Surrender your all
Get rid of your gall
Let God take the stand
Be in command

If you want to know peace
You need to release
Your fears and your doubt
To really find out

Trust in His word
Though it may seem absurd
He'll be faithful and true
To see your way through

Pure Through and Through

It takes strength and will
You must be still
Take control of your thoughts
Heaven can't be bought

Lighten your load
Be daring, be bold
Come in from the cold
Hard light of the day
Learn how to pray

He will hear you say,
"Come unto me.
Set me free.
Tell me how
To take hold of the plough.
I want to be free.
I want to be me."

In darkness or light
Continue to fight
Till you reach the end
Do not bend

On your promises true
Even when you are blue
Or forsaken it seems
It's all but a dream

When you awake
It will be for His sake
And not your own will
You have learned to be still

To look inwards to God
To Him you will nod
To find Him at last
Is really quite a blast

All karma you've burned
His love you have earned
He's made you brand new
Pure through and through

Real Love

Christ gave His life
As a ransom for man
I dare you to copy Him
Try if you can

Then you will know
What real love can do
But you won't know the answer
Until you are through

With all of the games
In His cosmic show
That keep you running
To and fro

You won't know yourself
When you partake of His wealth
His wisdom and glory
Then you'll know His story

Of how He meant for us to live
Not quoting the scriptures
But to give and to give

If you want to be free
Not bound by the law
The decrees and ethics
You have only to find
Your God-given path
And the right method
Of contacting Him
So you blunder no more
Hasten your journey
To heaven's door

Road to Glory

You've got to believe
Have faith in your heart
Before you depart
That's the key to the story
That leads you to glory

Trust in His word
You'll fly free as a bird
With nothing to lose
Except those old shoes
That you've outgrown
Once the seed is sown

Throw them away
That's the price
You must pay
His yoke is easy
His burden light
It's such a delight

Try it and see
What life can be
If He takes charge
You'll be able to barge
On the road up ahead
Leave behind your bed
Of heartache and pain
You have so much to gain

He'll give you His all
Even when you fall
Just answer His call
Forsake all the rest
To pass His test

Satan's Lie

Don't believe Satan
That you'll die in your sin
Jesus still loves you
He beckons, "Come in.

"Come sit at my table,
Partake of my grace,
All those who are weary
Of the battles they face."

Satan is a liar
He wants you to think
Your sins are too great,
So he makes a big stink

About going to hell,
Where you'll rot and burn,
If *his* love you spurn.

Hold yourself up;
Keep your head high.
Jesus does hear you
When you cry
To Him for His help;
He hears your deep sigh.

Have faith in His wisdom;
Don't lean on your own.
He has promised
To carry us home.

You must know the difference
'Tween God and the devil;
You must walk the path
On the straight and level

Highway to heaven,
Till you get past the door.
Then kiss Satan goodbye
For evermore.

Satan's Pleasures

They think it's absurd
To renounce Satan's pleasures;
They think they are treasures
To be counted and measured.

By how much can be bought?
They are so fraught
With keeping them safe,
Out of harm's way,
But come what may,
God will step in
Someday, somehow,
He'll call them forth
To put their hand to the plough.

If they refuse,
Prefer to snooze,
He'll remain silent;
He is so valiant.

A man of valour
A man of great worth,
Who can lead us to
A second birth.

We have to walk boldly
On the road up ahead,
Or become lost and dead
To His tender care;
Then alone we must bear

The burdens we created,
Or become sated
With Satan's pleasures
That seem like treasures.

Strength and Sight

There's no man alive
Who could not survive
All the battles of life
That give him much strife

'Cept he take up the plough
Learn to know how
To dig in the soil
Never recoil
From the hardships and pain
That still remain

From one life to the next
They're only a pretext
Of the good times ahead
No more need be said

It's a given
When we're driven
We'll correct all the wrongs
Set them all right
It takes inner-strength
And clear sight
Not force and great might

Sweet Mystery

Now that I'm wiser
I won't be a miser
In reclaiming my soul
From Satan's big hole
That he dug for me
Trying to keep me
From Thee

I'll continue to climb
To that life sublime
Forsake Satan's plan
He is the "big scam"
I'll see all was for naught
My life You have bought

It's no joke as they say
Those saints that did pray
For deliverance on high
They reached for the sky

So I will too
I want to be true
To my undying love
For You

I'll partake of Your life
Freer of strife
In the tree planted for me
In the sweet mystery

Thank You, Dear Master

For me, you are a masterpiece
One I would like to lease
To live in joy and ecstasy
From now until eternity

You taught us all
To be ever mindful
Of the fall
From your grace
Your teachings so true
Ones that were meant
To see us through

With little or nothing to regret
If only we would not forget
The great laws that are written
Not to be smitten
By sloth and by slander
Or when we should wander
Out of the range
Of your tender care
We should not dare

When we've learned
Our lessons well
You will remove
The dark Maya spell
That Satan has cast
Upon our lives
Upon which he thrives

Dear master, dear friend
May we not contend
To have our way
Because you see the play
Our part in this show
You can help us to grow
Dodge all the blows

If we only surrender
To the great sender
Of love, peace, and truth
From His heavenly booth

My guru, my master
I cannot grow faster
That what you plan for me
So I can be free

One day to roam
In my heavenly home
With you by my side
There to abide
In love ever after
Thank you, dear master!

Thank You Sis

I thank you for the times we spent
Throughout the years as I lay bent
Burdened with problems, sorrow and pain
You helped to ease them so I could remain

True to myself and God's given plan
I thank Him for each and every man
Who helped to see me through the maze
Those times when I was in a daze

I knew not where I was heading for
As I lay crying on the floor
For Him to rescue me from my plight
Give me wings for a brand new flight

Now here I am in a brand new land
It's thanks to you that I can stand
Upon my feet, smile and laugh
At all those pranks, wiles, and gaffs
That the devil played on me
As I was trying to break free

Your love and friendship I recall
Even when I was so small
And through the years
It's grown much stronger
Until I had to leave for yonder

Pastures that I knew not then
But here I am at home again
In a place that is right for me
Living who I wanted to be

I'm sorry for the hardship and woes
That caused me to give off blows
Of anger and heartaches
For leaving behind
Those that always were so kind

It was not easy to have to leave
To my family I did cleave
Until I found my place at last
And was able to be free from my past

In my heart you will remain
Forever a friend who kept me sane
When all around was crashing down
I thought of you
And your love so true

So please accept my apologies
That I offer on bended knee
In hopes that one day we both shall meet
And it will seem like quite a treat
Instead of the anger, sorrow, and pain
Because I could not by your side remain

I know not what the future holds
Only that life will unfold
With each new passing, glorious day
As I remember to get down and pray
Thank God for the goodness
That has come into my life
That has helped to alleviate some of the strife

Now it's no longer up to you
To help me through
For I am able to get up off the floor
And make my way
God has opened the door

To a new and better life in BC
In time I'm sure that you will see
That all has happened for the better
Even though it didn't fit to the letter

It feels right for me, finally
So please accept my heartfelt decree
That you have helped to set me free
Now I can live, free to be me!

The Big Chill

All they can do is shudder,
When God forbid you utter
Or mention His name.
They think you're insane.

"Never mind," they say.
"I have done it myself.
His name I prefer
To put on the shelf.

"What I see is what I get.
I ain't seen Him yet.
So I'm not laying a bet,
There's someone bigger,
Better than me.
I'm at ease, I'm in love,
I'm content as can be."

Till the day they wake up
See they failed to sup
When the Lord came a calling
They were all bawling
Because they passed Him by
For some pie in the sky.

For more of life's fancies
Because they were antsy
For another thrill
That promised "big chill"
Only to find
They're at the end of the line.

Only some will recall
That He is their all
Sitting on the throne
Calling them home.

The Broken Link

Our thoughts must be pure
Without any taint
Take heart, do not worry
Don't be discouraged
Don't faint

With each passing trial
You'll get rid of denial
You'll learn to surrender
Instead of going on a bender

You'll gain control
Of your mind
And your feelings
These can't be bought
They must be sought
With self-knowledge and strength
You must go to great length
Put fear on the shelf
To conquer the self

No man can purchase
These gems with his money
With flattery or wine
His thoughts must be Mine

Not what your brother
Or neighbour should speak
My truth I have planted
In your heart to seek

In quiet and solitude
Not gossip and talk
Let no man balk
At the depths of My word
Let no man say,
"They are absurd."

Surely he knows not
The error of his ways
When calamity falls
And he is swayed
To transgress his good conscience
The depths of My love
When wisdom falls short and
He takes flight like the dove

That has lost its home
In the sycamore tree
And broken the link
Between you and Me

The Creator

Will they know it is You, Lord?
They have been seeking
Through all of this maze,
Which has kept them in a daze.

What will they say?
When they find they were blind
That they worshipped themselves,
Or the books on their shelves,
The priests and the prophets
All them that "got it".

When will they learn
To get down on their knees,
Bow to You
The author, the maker,
The great Creator?

The Devil in Disguise

Ah, but for that devil in disguise,
Who is always planning my demise,
But to his surprise,
I have become wise.

I've been around
That corner before;
I've been on death's door
Maybe four score and more.

It's become my habit
To check in and see
What the good Lord
Wants from me.

When I plan a move
Or make a call,
I have to ask,
"Is this the fall
That the devil has taken
From his bag
To make me look
Like the ugly old scrag?"

The one who is out
To bring him to earth,
From his lofty perch
Whence he gave birth
To that haughty grimace
He wears on his face,
His chest all puffed up
Hiding his disgrace.

From all his misdeeds
That I know so well,
You see they were born
With him in hell.

For hell is what
We make of our lives
Here on earth,
When we deny
That love of Christ
And his gift of mirth
That was given birth,
When He died for us all
After the fall
Of Adam and Eve,
Whom the devil deceived.

And ever after
We've been the captors
Of our own sinful ways,
When instead we should pray:

"Lord, deliver us from evil
So that our days will be spent
In living and loving You,
Not worrying about
Some extravagant rent.

"That only breeds contempt
From those less fortunate
Who have only tin walls,
No toilet to pee in,
Only a stall

"In the yard or the alley
Where the insects all rally,
To poison their victims
With fiery darts
That come from that devil
Or one of his upstarts."

He has so many tricks
In that big bag of his.
Don't try to outsmart him
He knows his showbiz.

He's taken me on
Many a long walkabout,
And I went right along
With not even a pout.

For I knew that I took
Along in my bag
One who was greater
About whom I could brag.

The one who allows me
To stand, sit, or walk,
On those tiresome journeys
When I could not even talk.

So silent was I,
Under his cruel demise.
His pranks and tricks
I did despise.
So I often sat down
And had a good cry.

I cried to the Lord
To have mercy on me
Take me back home,
Set me free.

But each time He set me
Back on the path
To show that devil
His Holy wrath.

For worshipping self
And all of his wealth,
For passing the stranger
Who was in grave danger.

As he went on his way
Secure in his castle
That was built of clay,
And will fade one day.

His bridges he burnt
From his selfish moves,
Which held others in want
So he could prove

He was king of his castle,
No need for another,
Not even his mother
Who bore and raised him
From birth to adulthood.
Behind him she stood

With fingers worked
Right to the bone,
Hoping one day
He would phone home,

To see how she was doing
While she sat alone,
Nursing the memories
Of when he was a boy;
How she scraped to buy him
A brand new toy.

Or a new pair of shoes
That fit him just right,
Hoping he wouldn't
Get into a fight

With the kids on the block
Or the girls next door,
When he didn't get his candy
From the corner store.

They're not all dressed in red
With two horns and a trident,
But they're hell bent on self
And all of their wealth.

All the money they spend,
Buying their treasures,
For their own pleasure,
That one day will fade,
As sure as God made
The sun in the sky.
But they don't know why
Or even ask
What it means to fast.
They're used to satiety
And not sobriety.

They don't know how
To find peace in their heart.
They're used to pulling
The bullock cart.

When God's yoke is easy,
His burden is light;
He's just waiting for them
To welcome Him in
To His shelter on high
All their tears He will dry.

This world is the devil's
Playground of ploys
Full of fancy, expensive toys.

All manner of hatred
Jealousy and scorn,
For he knows that
Man was born
To be free from it all.
So the devil created
All the brawls

That keep men entangled,
From one life to the next,
Under such a pretext
That they can hardly believe
They need to take leave

Of this dream world of ours,
Where we spend hours and hours
Trying to decipher
Without a Holy miter,
What life's all about.

When we only need shout,
Sing praises to Him,
To free us from sin,
Then the devil
Can't get in.

There will be
No place in our hearts
For other than God,
Upon whose earth we trod
To make our way
Back home to His throne
We are never alone.

But Satan likes
To keep us in doubt,
Always wondering
When we will get out.
Where did we come from?
And whence we return?
He knows it's God's love
We have spurned.

By now we should have
Heeded the call,
Above them all,
But we insist instead
In making our bed.

Then lie in it we must,
As we make a great fuss,
When things turn out sour
Hour after hour.

We know not that peace
That comes from His hand,
A peace so strong
That we can withstand
All the wiles of the devil,
In which he revels.

He's after our souls.
He's made it his goal
To be king of his realm
With him at the helm,
While we live in hell
As he casts his spell
On our misery making
For our forsaking
That peace that passes
All understanding.
God's love is demanding.

And that's where Satan
Comes into play,
That men's minds
He may sway

Away from the heart,
Straight to the head,
So he can keep us
On his bed
Of pain and sorrow,
Failure and deceit.
He is "The Big Cheat!"

So up the mighty banner
Of God's love we must hold.
It's the same old story,
One that's been told
From time immemorial;
The good and the bad
The light and the dark
The happy and the sad.

Don't wait till tomorrow
To let Him come in.
You'll drown in your sorrow,
Go deeper in sin.

Take a moment right now;
Put your hand to the plough.
Dig deep in the soil;
Do not recoil.
For it's never too late
To open the gate
Of heaven's glory.
Let it be your story!

The Divine Plan

Let's do all we can
To find the Divine plan
According to His will
Then He'll pay the bill

We'll rest in His arms
Safe from all harm
Knowing that He
Our happiness dost see
Better than we
Can ever predict
But He may have to
Use the stick
Of hardship and pain
For His kingdom to gain
But then we'll remain
In His kingdom forever
The chains He will sever

The Dying Game

Oh, collect calls he made
Over the years from Columbia,
But they were all mumbled
With liquor and cursing,
From the bottle he was nursing
Trying to forget all the
Heartache and pain
Of his sorrowful childhood,
Which he inflicted again

On those who stood by him
For better or worse,
But dig in his pocket
Or get out his purse,
By golly, it was like
Pulling out teeth,
Only worse for the asking
Because you nearly got a wreath

Around your neck,
So you'd remember
He was on a bender,
And never recalled
All the fights
And the brawls.

The worst of it all
Is he bragged all the time,
How he didn't have a dime
But he was living in luxury,
Riding on fame,
Amassing his fortune,
His ill-gotten gains.

It meant nothing to him
To spend time in the pen.
"You do the crime,
You do the time.

"I have years ahead of me,
Fortunes galore,
Just waiting for freedom
To knock at my door.

"Won't be long now
'Fore I finish this out.
I carry a gun and
Carry great clout!"

I shudder to think
Of the demise that's in store
For a man who tells lies
The same evermore.

For there is no room
In his mixed-up head.
He likes to control
Or else you are dead.

He likes to tell you
Where, when, and how,
And you better
"Get it now!"

He's done it over
And over to us;
Always making
A great big fuss.

He doesn't seem to know
Wrong from right,
He just keeps on harping,
Keeps up the fight.

It's sad, it's a pity,
It's darn right cruel.
What is one to do?
But let an old fool

Die is his misery,
Fortune and fame.
I want no part of
The dying game.

The End of the Line

I don't mind
When You scold me
For I have learned
You are Holy

It's when I wander
From Your ways
That I get lost
In Satan's play

Of right and wrong
To his delight
He likes to put up
Quite a fight

Now I know
That all is You
I cannot help but
See them through
All the Maya
You did spread
Upon this earth
Until we're dead

Dead to this world
And all its charms
It was never meant
To do us harm

It's only a part
Of Your magical spell
But Satan wants
To take us to hell

You planned it all
Right from the start
To try us and test us
To open our hearts
To see who we'll find
When we finally get
To the end of the line

The Forest

I went for a walk in the forest today,
To see what the good Lord
Had to say.

Lo and behold,
He showed me a brook,
That flowed ever onward
Into each little nook
And cranny that wound
Through the winding ravines;
It flowed ever onward,
Without bursting its seams.

He said, "That is how life
Is meant to be:
Flowing ever onward
Until we are free.

"Free from the fetters
That cling to our soul,
Unbound and unhindered,
Cleansed and whole."

Then I spotted the wild flowers
Beside the way.
He said, "Jane, do not pick them;
They're here to stay.
Their roots have dug deep
Into the fertile soil.
If you pull them up,
They will recoil.

"Their colourful presence
I have designed;
Their sweet smelling fragrance
Is so sublime.

"That is how life
Is meant to be:
Rooted in the fragrance
Of a life lived for Me!"

The Heart is the Knower

The heart is the knower
Of the things that are hidden,
Things we may want but
For our sake
Forbidden.

Those things that we long for
That give us no peace
Are meant for the stockpile
They were just a fleece,
To lead us ever onward
On our journey back home,
Where God in His goodness
Will sit on the throne.

The Honour of a Father

He said he loved me
Through and through,
That he would be there
When I was blue,

When I was sick,
When I had wealth,
When I was distant,
Put on the shelf
To suffer for my inattention
To his lusts
And new inventions.

But none of them
Came true you see,
For he was not looking
Back at me.

He only saw
The blue sky above,
Forgot about
His undying love

That he professes
To this day,
But Lord, help him
Should he have to pay?

For all his misdeeds
His errors, his might,
He likes to put up
Quite a fight.

For his rights you see
Were more important than me
Or the kids that we bore
"I'll love them," he swore,

As he ran out the door
And chose to ignore
He once tied the knot;
All this he forgot:
The responsibility and honour
Of being a good father.

The Lying Game

The lies, they pierce holes
Straight through your heart,
Which can only be mended
With a brand new start.

They say that they love you
Then walk out the door,
To pastures much greener,
You've become quite a bore.

With your faith and hope
In an invisible God,
Upon whose earth
You've always trod.

They know not His ground
Is more hallowed and sound
Than the footsteps that run
Up the road of wrong doing;
Satan even delights
In the one he is suing.

For no other reason
Than to satisfy his lust,
A winner he must be
Or you'll bite the dust.

It's Satan who's lying
In wait for his bait:
Those who harbour hatred
And deceit at their gates.

He loves to get
Inside their minds,
From behind
Closed doors of jealousy,
Anger and lust.
They're just a few
Of his musts.

He's the trickster sublime.
He's had plenty of practice.
Just cling to the Lord.
Don't mind his antics.

For the bottomless pit
Is filled to the brim,
With creatures of horror
Who are rank with great sin

That they've not confessed
But buried in shame,
Or maybe in pride,
Playing Satan's lying game.

You'll not want to go there,
To the pit of despair,
Instead put your trust
In the Lord; it's a must.

Then you will enter
His home by and by,
With the wings of an angel
And a great big sigh.

With truth in your heart,
You'll be ready to start
A new life in time,
Even more sublime

Than the one you just lived,
Which has vanished like
Sand through a sieve,
Sifting through time
And space with no rhyme.

When you've humbled yourself
And are thirsting anew
For justice and truth,
God will see you through.

The Master Craftsman

When you've met the Master
Craftsman of life
Who created the strife
That'll lead us all home
To his heavenly throne

You'll praise God for His mercies
His hardships and pain
They were meant for our gain
Not lasting sorrow
But a better tomorrow

The angels will greet you
As you stand at the door
Never to return
To earth's lonely shore

His peace and His wisdom
You won't want to miss
You'll be filled to the brim
With His ephemeral bliss

The Mountain

He created the mountain
As a symbol to climb
To His life sublime
So tarry no more
At the base
Seek the summit
Or you will plummet
To depths untold

The story's been told
With each passing age
Become as the prophets
One like a sage

Who carries within him
That golden cup
Of trials and burdens
But never gave up

The lessons he learned
Redeemed his soul
He made life ever after
His eternal goal

The Pearl

I dreamed I was
In rivers deep
When I awoke
I realized I was only
Fast asleep

Dreaming life's
Enchanting ways
It's good for others
So they say

A little dip and you will find
The pearl, the stone
Inside the rind

But I did not dig
Deep enough
The road is long
The way is rough

The pearl, it can be only found
When you are walking
On hallowed ground

So I sent a cry to God on high
For some new way
To view life's journey
This I prayed:

"Lord, teach me how
To be at peace
With friend and foe
That wherever I go
My hand I can reach
To those who slumber
To those who preach
'Bout life's enchanting dream
That carries them
Headlong down the stream
On tides and waves
Of troubles and woes
They know not how
The story goes."

So I dove again
This time for the jetty
Even though
It seemed quite petty

Then lo, the bars that stood
Outside my door
Vanished from sight
For evermore

The Poor and the Lonely

God already knew
How it would be on that day
So He planned how to pay
For the poor and the lonely
For the broken of heart
He'd give them a new start

Where their needs are all met
Where they don't need to sweat
To earn their keep
Or follow like sheep
To the slaughter
They can tend to their daughter
Their other children of light
For them He will fight

That's what He's promised
To those who love Him
For those who don't
The story's quite grim

They will find out
When their luck runs out
Then they will know
To whom to turn
So they can sow
The good seeds of wisdom
Truth and real love
Hopefully it will be
To the good Lord above

The Promised Land

That's all I ask
That I have You
I've done it all
I've seen men fall
But I still stood tall
Waiting and watching
For Your gentle hand
To lead me to
The Promised Land.

Of peace of joy
Of happiness replete
I let them all
Strive and compete
For fame and fortune
Possessions galore
Till I found them
Quite a bore.

When I tried
To talk of You
They rolled their eyes
Made me blue
With faces askew.

"Why would I need Him?"
They would say
But there'll come a day
When the tides will turn
And they will learn
To reach out and pray
For that glorious day.

When all their wants
And desires are stilled
Their dreams and wonders
Are fulfilled.

That Promised Land
Where man can stand
Safe in Your arms
Free from all harm.

The Refrain

.

So happy am I
When I hold my head high
Don't look around
Or wear that sad frown
Of longings and regrets
That only beset
Us with sorrow and pain
We have nothing to gain
When we get caught in the refrain of
"A life lived for me,
Instead of for Thee!"

The Seer of All

Hatred doth blind
The heart with shame
Jealousy it doth remain
Till it strikes like a deer
Running with great fear

Fear for your life
All you've acquired
Maybe you should have
Dug deep in the mire

Of the quicksand you're in
While you're in a tailspin
Harbouring those feelings
Of guilt and doubt
Trying to figure it all out

Get the mind out of the way
Come back inside
Your hatred, your jealousy
You cannot hide

It shows on your face
In your eyes in the mirror
In the one who's before you
He is the seer

The seer of all
To help you recall
Your God-given image
Get rid of the scrimmage

Let love reign in your heart
Do your part
Then the seer of all
Will not let you fall

The Spirit Three

Born from a seed
From our mother's birth
Only to return
To Mother Earth
With such great mirth

Only a soul would know
Who has reached the goal
Of union with self
With only the wealth
Of his soul set free
By the spirit three

The Still of the Night

The mists that arise
In the cool night skies
Fall gently upon me
Setting me free

Like a refreshing rain
That soothes away pain
Washes me clean
With the soft moonbeam

That shines from above
With Divine Mother's love
Bringing healing from sorrow
For a better tomorrow

The Thrill of it All

Maybe they like
The thrill of it all
They're often quite like that
Those men that are small

In stature and mind
Some day they will find
That they will all fall
From their perches on high
With not even a sigh
Of regret or remorse
That they took
The wrong course

Some never change
They remain as antiques
That you put on the shelf
Some call them freaks

The White Pearly Gates

Surely you don't understand
What He means by
The "Promised Land"

That perpetual joy
That lights up your soul
Making you happy, carefree
And whole

Alive each new day
To take on come what may
For you know in the end
It is He that did send

All the trials and darkness
The joys and the sorrows
Leading us on to
A better tomorrow

If only we trust in His
Guiding right hand
He'll not let us down
When we think we can't stand

Up to our enemy
Without giving flight
To our tears and torments
To our painful plight

When our tears turn to rivers
That wind and that bend
They help see us through
To our journey's end

God does not dictate
Manage or fuss
Our path is wide open
It's left up to us

To make our way straight
To His white pearly gates

They're Part of You

God has allowed me
To live not in vain,
But I certainly haven't
Lived up to my name.

"Plain Jane"
They have ribbed me
From when I was small,
But I just walked proudly
Straight down the hall

Of those long, lonely corridors
Of boredom and rules,
Of my seventeen years
That I was in school.

Lo and behold
I was princess at last,
In my final school year,
But they knew not my past.

Those dark, tearful nights
That I lay on my bed,
Praying to Jesus
Somehow I'd be fed

If I struck out alone
On His path carved for me.
It was all that I wanted:
Just to be me.

I hung around
With sinners and saints,
But in my soul
There was no taint

Of malice or spite
I just thought,
"All men are right."

They all perceived
From their own narrow view.
How could I judge them,
When they're part of You?

This Very Hour

When we try to replace Him
With people, places, and things
In hopes that good tidings
These would bring

The loneliness remains
To keep us in chains
As before
Because we have blatantly
Closed the door

To His tender love
His will and His power
That would have kept us
From this very hour

When we hearken to change
Come within His range
He can take over
Then like a four-leaf clover

Our luck will grow stronger
As our thoughts turn yonder
To His kingdom, His power
That will guide us each hour

He won't let us down
He'll give us the crown
Of justice and mercy
The will to do right
He'll never let us
Out of His sight

Those Prison Bars

It was one of my biggest
Decisions in life:
How to tell my children
And not cause them strife?

When I broke the news
That their dad was in prison,
My daughter cried,
My son mused.
I knew they were confused.

But that was not
The end of story;
It got quite gory.

My son became sorry;
He tried to take
His precious life
With pills galore
He bought at the store.

Then my daughter
Cut her wrists,
Her dear old dad
She surely missed.

She took some pills
And drank some gin;
The story got quite grim.

―――――――

Both times I sped
To their hospital bed,
With them I pled
For them to hang on,
Get back on their feet.
It wasn't such a terrible feat.

To have their dad
Behind prison bars
I told them both
He was safer by far

Than roaming the streets
With the drug cartel.
Prison might keep him
From going to hell.

Thou Shalt be Clean

My bones are achy
So brittle and dry
It's for my soul's good
So I need not cry

The Lord, He is working
Deep down in my soul
To remove all the blemishes
Make me whole

By whole I mean
Enjoined to Him
Free from tarnishes
Free from sin

It's no wonder that
I ache and pant
Like a war-torn soldier
That is ready to supplant

His life unto death
Just like Macbeth
But not for some treason
He has His reason

It depends on the depths
Of the cleansing it takes
To right all the wrongs
That I must forsake

God knows the ones
That are hard to remove
It could take awhile
For His sweet reprove

They've been there forever
Controlling my mind
I could not fathom
That I was so blind

However those thoughts
Came to rule in my heart
He's refining the process
They must depart

For His thoughts to enter
He must be the centre
Of all of our musings
The great and the small
He must be our all

So I'll rejoice in the refining
Instead of fine dining
For the feast that I'll find
Is a treasure sublime

One I'll never regret
Once my heart is set
On reaching the goal
Of becoming cleansed
And whole

Thy Will be Done

For me there is
Only one way
Thy will be done
Come what may

Other voices do impede
Knowing my wants
From my needs
Sometimes I do get
All mixed up
In my haste
Your plans disrupt

No matter how hard
I have to struggle
All the plans
I have to juggle
I'll change them each day
If that's what You say
I'll listen for a clue
Till I know
It's from You

Teach me to
Stay calm and pray
For Your guidance
Your strength each day

Together We'll Stand

I want you to be
The face that I see
When I arise
With the morning sunrise
My guru, my friend,
My lover, till the end

I'll heed them not
In Satan's great plot
To take me away
From the part I must play
In joining with you
Make my dream come true

Together we'll stand
We'll walk hand in hand
As you carry me home
To heaven's throne

Trust in His Word

It's every fall
I do recall
You beckoned me
To come fly free

To play in Your game
One of spirit
Not might
You showed me how to
Stand up and fight

The fall I left
For Bonaventure
My, oh my
It was quite the adventure
A ride I'll never forget
On that you can bet

Before I left
I read Your word
'Bout the lilies of the field
The birds in the air
Who had no care

I needn't worry
'Bout food or drink
What clothes to wear
I had only to think

And lo, You'd be there
To supply my needs
My every desire
It was then You set
My heart on fire

I tried and tested Your every word
Even when it seemed absurd

Be it wood or fruit
Or a brand new suit
A job or money
And even honey
It was so funny!
You supplied it all
I do recall

It was a shining example
Of my walk with the Lord
I couldn't believe
All the ways I had scored

───────────

The best was the
Little car stereo
When I was feeling
Rather low
My neighbor found it in her shed
I was nearly out of my head
For music fills my soul you see
With thoughts and dreams
Of You and me

My neighbours were
So kind to me
They even brought me
A Christmas tree

My mother came and
Shared in the spoils
The neighbours thought
She was so royal

I painted the house
From top to bottom
Though the floors and doors
Were nearly rotten

Our big, red jalopy
Looked kind of sloppy
So the kids would hide
When we would ride
Around the town
They would frown
But hey, it was free
They were embarrassed
But not me

We skied and picnicked
Winter and summer
But the old house sold
It was a bummer

It was just the beginning
Of my walk with the Lord
I can tell you for certain
I was never bored

God was faithful and true
Each step of the way
He delivered on His promises
In a powerful way

Trust in You

You gave us birth
To live on earth
Transcend the world view
Come home to You

Where life is so sweet
As we sit at Your feet
With our troubles and woes
Where You take the blows
Of our worldly endeavours
You are so clever

You planned the plot
That has tied its great knot
In our story untold
It will unfold
As we place trust in You
To see our way through

Watching Over Me

Our journey, He planned
Right from the start
He planted it secretly
Deep in our heart
He's patiently waiting
For us to see
He's been there forever
Watching over
You and me

Way Over His Head

For years I kept taking
That tiny yellow pill
Praying and meditating
And the voices stilled

So I thought I was better
Till I got the letter
From that violent man
Who was my ex
I thought it was he
Who had given the hex

On my life for departing
From his cruel embrace
His company and yelling
I could not face

For he shouts all the time
That he hasn't a dime
To spare for us three
While he barks up a tree
That he has millions aside
That he has to hide

We'll never know
Because he treats us as foes
Professing his love
But giving us woes

He won't share his riches
Except with those women
He now calls bitches
Because they put him out
Just like I did
And now he's living
Alone on the skid
But full of great fame
As he brags how he won
Playing in the game

Of drugs and guns
Killing and bandits
Of pirates and gold
All them that "have it"

You never know
From one day to the next
If he's going to behead you
Or give you the hex

When he tells me his stories
Some are real gory
I can't listen too much
But he doesn't shut up

His story reminds me
Of the long lost son
Who is lost in the battle
That must be won

The unsolved traumas
The mystery dramas
That plague us through life
Causing much strife

I think he got in
Way over his head
And has to play dead
Just to stay alive
That's how he survives

When They Reach Heaven

We should all learn
To laugh at the crowds
That live life carelessly
Happy and proud
Of all their endeavours
Their fortunes and fame
When they reach heaven
Will He call them by name?

No. He'll assign them a mansion
Not fit for a queen
He'll ask them one question,
"Where the hell have you been?

"Wandering in darkness
Through tempest like stones
When all of this time
I was calling you home.

"Home to your inner castle
Of peace and joy
Don't you know, dear friend
They just used you as a toy?

"Something to play with
Till they're really fed up,
Then throw you away
For a brand new cup.

"Of pleasure and venture
With no end in sight.
Truly it's a sorrowful,
Ungodly plight."

You Did it All

My Lord, My God
My feet are shod
With Thy grace
Within my heart
You called my name
Right from the start

When I was still
Inside the womb
You planned mansions for me
Not a stone tomb

You called me to fly free
In a life lived for Thee

It is You who's been there
From beginning to end
Let me not tarry
Lament or pretend

I have any great riches
Gifts that are mine
They all come from You
The one who is Divine

I'll not live in vain
With nothing to gain
It's You that I want
You are the font
Let me ever recall
You did it all

You Hold Us Dear

When we finally get home
To sit on His throne
We'll know all the answers
We'll be godly dancers
Who dance, sing, and shout
There'll be no more doubt
Only one happy refrain,
"Lord, let's do it again!"

So we can reclaim
The lost and the lonely
Who know not Your love
Was conceived
In the heavens above

It was brought down to earth
To fill it with mirth
Peace and contentment
Not boredom and resentment
Hatred and lust
Anger and fear
You hold us dear

You'll Never Get Home

Courageous are those
Who fight that foe
That deals its blow
Time and again
Much to man's
Sorrowful chagrin

There's no turning back
You gotta take up the slack
Put the self of the shelf
Share your wealth
Or fall from your
"Garden of Eden"
You're creating
Make it one
Where God is partaking

He must be the one
To sit on your throne
Or you'll never get in there
You'll never get home

Your Claim to Fame

Change is a constant
While we're here on earth
It leads us to
Our second birth

We can never stand still
You beckon us ever
To new heights and vistas
You are so clever

To tailor our journey
To our own special needs
It is You who is constantly
Planting the seeds

Our successes and failures
They're all just a game
In our remarkable journey
It's Your claim to fame

Your Love

It's only because
I took shelter in You
That I was able
To see my way through

Without Your love
Your constant care
Your word, Your guidance
I could not have dared

To endure all the trials
You set before me
I learned to do it
On bended knee

With no bread on the table
No job close at hand
I chose You instead, Lord
I learned how to stand

With my head held high
My heart breaking so
From those broken-down promises
From friend and foe

Without that humble
Contrition of heart
We soon find out
We're right back at the start

If only we'd learn
To play in the game
Do it for You, Lord
With no thought of gain

No other reliance
Than help from above
You'll always stand by us
Show us Your love

Your Smile

(To my friend Sally)

You have a smile
That lights up the world
With the innocence of youth
With wisdom unfurled

It's a smile that shines brightly
From the depths of the self
Illuminating the world
With joy and the wealth

Of someone who knows
Her very own soul
Of someone who's made happiness
A lofty goal

From joy we come
In joy we move
In joy we have our being
Now you are seeing

Through eyes that shine brightly
Like diamonds and pearls
With a luminous smile
That lights up the world

Your Touch

I sorely resented
Your touch at times
It seemed so severe
Still, You held me near

I tried to do
What You advised
Although some deeds
I did despise
But in the end
Your tender mercies
You did send

When I took shelter
From the storms
From the battles of life
With all its strife

I became like the tree
Planted by the waters
So still
Until I had my fill
Was once again free:
Free to be me

About The Author

Jane Thompson is an avid yoga and meditation teacher, reflexologist, numerologist, volunteer supporting women's rights against violence, mental health advocate, hospice worker, and world traveler.

Jane was born to travel. After a cross-Canada/U.S. tour in her early teens, and several European vacations as a teenager, Jane's passion for life, her inquisitive mind, and her courageous spirit led her on a two-year, round-the-world adventure at the age of 20. During her eight-year marriage, she and her husband toured Canada, Australia, and the Caribbean. A yoga enthusiast from her early thirties, Jane realized a long held dream when she explored India—the Motherland of religion and yoga—during a three-month spiritual pilgrimage more recently.

Jane attributes her travels, a difficult upbringing, and a turbulent marriage, to her spiritual thirst for the deeper meaning of life. Having overcome a mental illness herself, Jane has developed an innate understanding of the effects of trauma on the human psyche; this healing journey has enabled her to transcend the powers of darkness with the grace so befitting of her birth name, Jane (meaning God's grace).

When Jane studied World Religions at Concordia University in Montreal in the early eighties, she marveled at truths found in the Hindu scriptures, and their parallels with her own Christian faith. She then discovered the teachings of her beloved guru, Paramahansa Yogananda, and awakened to the transcendent truth that lies at the heart of life's mysteries. At 36, upon completing yoga teacher training at the Sivananda Ashram in Val Morin, Quebec, Swami Vishnudevananda conferred on her the spiritual title, Sri Devi. Twelve years later, at the age of 48, she embarked in earnest on the Kriya Yoga path as taught by Yoganada.

Sri Devi believes that time, forgiveness, unconditional love, faith, prayer, and meditation are our healers—forever leading us toward the eternal goal of Self-realization. In her eyes, times of joy, sorrow, failure, success, work, rest, birth, and death are all fundamental components of the law of relativity that comprise our spiritual struggle to evolve, to improve, to transform, and ultimately, to seek and to know one's Maker. She is convinced that when we love God, and when we are in tune with His will, the dreams that we dare to dream really do come true. In this anthology of lyrical poems, Sri Devi urges us to attune to Divine Will and to its subsequent blessings.

Sri Devi is a proud, devoted mother and grandmother to her two grown children and grandson. Born in Winnipeg, Manitoba, and raised in Montreal, Quebec, she is a nature lover at heart, and feels blessed by the natural beauty and peaceful surroundings of her home in Port Alberni, British Columbia, on the West Coast of Canada.

CPSIA information can be obtained
at www.ICGtesting.com
Printed in the USA
LVOW11s0510150317
527232LV00001B/10/P